Passive Sentences in English and Portuguese

Milton M. Azevedo

Georgetown University Press, Washington, D.C. 20057

Library of Congress Cataloging in Publication Data

Azevedo, Milton Mariano, 1942-
Passive sentences in English and Portuguese.

A revision of the author's thesis, Cornell University, 1973.
Bibliography: p.
1. Portuguese language--Passive voice.
2. Portuguese language--Syntax. 3. Portuguese language--Semantics. 4. English language--Passive voice. 5. English language--Syntax. 6. English language--Semantics. 7. Portuguese language--Grammar, Comparative--English. 8. English language--Grammar, Comparative--Portuguese. I. Title.
PC5151.A98 1979 415 79-24987
ISBN 0-87840-078-8

Printed in the United States of America

International Standard Book Number: 0-87840-078-8

CONTENTS

Para Frederick B. Agard,
mestre e amigo

INTRODUCTION

This study is intended as a description of passivization in Portuguese and English and a contrastive analysis of the main types of passive constructions in the two languages. The parameters adopted for the descriptive analysis are the semantic characterization of the elements participating in the formation of the sentences, the processes by which passives are generated, and the relationships between passivization and the distribution of the information contained in the semantic structure, along the linearized surface representation. The order in which these parameters have been listed reflects what is assumed here to be an appropriate hierarchy of problems in language description and an order of priorities which seems to have won a degree of credence in linguistics during the last decade or so.

The development of linguistics in the United States showed until recently an effort to establish clear-cut limits to what should constitute the proper object of the discipline. Between the thirties and the late fifties, before transformational-generative analysis came into the scene, American linguists were largely concerned with problems of phonology and morphology. Syntax was studied principally under variations of immediate constituent analysis,[1] and semantics received minimal attention, as can be seen in an examination of the treatment of problems of meaning in introductory treatises written in those years.

For example, Gleason (1955, 1961) mentioned meaning mainly in connection with problems of the isolation, identification, and classification of phonological and morphological units. Hockett (1958:138ff.) characterized the semantic part of language as a peripheral system which 'associates various morphemes, combinations of morphemes, and arrangements in which morphemes can be put, with things and situations, or kinds of things and situations'. Hall (1964) devoted only a handful out of 470 pages to general considerations on meaning; while recognizing that 'semantics...forms the bridge between linguistics and the nonlinguistic world, and as such, although on the border line, forms an integral and essential part of linguistics', he maintained that 'in the analysis of linguistic structure...considerations of form must take precedence over considerations of meaning. These latter do play a role, but it must of necessity be a subordinate one' (Hall 1964:33).

During this period, authors generally favored the view that, although meaning was a very important part of language, its systematic study was at best extremely difficult, given the state of their discipline at the time. Gleason, for instance, thought it justifiable to exclude meaning from descriptive linguistics 'precisely because it is meaning in which we are ultimately interested' (1961:94). The use of semantic considerations in descriptive studies was apologetically tolerated as a heuristic device that was necessary because linguists were

> forced to use semantic criteria in trying to get at the grammatical system, for we have to discover, somehow, whether two utterances...'mean the same thing' or 'have different meanings' for the native speaker (Hockett 1958:138-139).

Linguistics devoted most of its attention to what Hockett (1958:137) called the 'central systems' of language, that is, phonology, morphology, and morphophonemics. This is evident in Harris' proposal (1955:191)[2] for a theory of linguistic analysis which made use of distributional procedures involving

> no reference to the meaning of morphemes--that is, no knowledge or judgment of meanings or meaning-differences, and no reliance on the speaker's ability to respond in terms of the meaning or meaning-differences of morphemes.

The theory of language outlined by Chomsky (1957) stated the primacy of syntax over other aspects of linguistic analysis and submitted that it was not only possible but also necessary that appeal to meaning should be left out of the construction of either a general theory of grammar or the grammar of an individual language. In brief, that hypothesis proposed a formal device that produced grammatically well-formed sentences, as if 'we were studying language as an instrument or a tool, attempting to describe its structure with no explicit reference to the way in which this instrument is put to use' (Chomsky 1957:103). The underlying assumption was that, whereas a formal basis could serve as a 'foundation for the construction of grammatical theory' (Chomsky 1957:100), a semantics-based one would be incapable of achieving equally satisfactory results. However, the study of meaning was not regarded as either unfeasible or beyond the proper interest of linguistics. What was implied was that semantic analysis could only be undertaken after the investigation of syntax had been sufficiently developed so as to contribute to it.[3] The study of semantics should be part of a more general theory of language than was then proposed, and this general theory should be capable of incorporating correlations between syntactic structure and meaning.

Although Chomsky's 1957 model was mainly concerned with syntax and only dealt with semantics in passing, it did point out the general directions which the study of meaning should follow. Semantic investigation should be based on the study of syntactical relations and should develop from the analysis of the correspondences between syntax and semantics. The study of such points of contact should be the object of a theory of language broad enough to include 'a theory of linguistic form and a theory of the use of language' (Chomsky 1957: 102).

An important attempt to construct a semantic theory along transformational-generative lines was presented by Katz and Fodor (1963), further developed by Katz and Postal (1964), and later endorsed by Chomsky (1965). This linguistic model preserved the notion of the centrality of syntax, and despite claims that it had been conceived not 'as an isolated system of principles but as an integrated part of a broader theory about the nature of language in general' (Katz and Martin 1967: 125), it offered a view of language in which the semantic component had a purely interpretive role. On the other hand, Katz and Fodor's 1963 work may be regarded as a statement on semantic metatheory rather than on the semantics of an individual language.[4]

The new semantic theory won both applause and criticism, but the fact that most relevant critiques were directed at the formalization of the theory itself (e.g. Bolinger 1965 and Chafe 1968), rather than at its fundamental concern with semantics, indicated that a number of linguists already accepted the feasibility of carrying out the study of meaning within the scope of their discipline. This renewed interest in problems of meaning has gradually led a number of scholars to the conclusion that syntactic structure is much more dependent on semantic structure than was previously believed to be the case. An examination of the literature reveals a development from an attempt at compromise between the view that semantics cannot be separated from syntax and the model of linguistic theory defended by Chomsky and his followers, on the one hand, and new approaches which reject the Chomskyan standard theory, on the other. One such alternate proposal was presented by Weinreich (1966) who explicitly maintained the Chomskyan (1965) format of the grammar and included, besides the base and the transformational subcomponent, the notion that transformations do not affect the meaning of sentences. One of the fundamental differences between interpretive semantics and Weinreich's model was that in the latter there is nothing like a semantic component postulated separately from the syntactic component. Since Weinreich's proposal tried to preserve most of the syntactic component as devised by Chomsky, it may be considered a transitional approach between interpretive semantics and generative semantics,[5] a school of thought which started as a dissident offshoot of the Chomskyan version of transformational grammar.

In the first major paper which gave indication of a split among transformational-generative linguists (Lakoff 1965), it was suggested that acceptance of a level of deep structure as was generally formulated at the time led to the establishment of a new sublevel of deep structure for each deep structure previously postulated. This resulted in the description becoming encumbered with an increasing number of underlying representations 'further removed from the superficial form of sentences than had been thought necessary' (McCawley 1969:15). Moreover, the final syntactic structures thus generated tended to be so similar to the semantic structures of the sentences being described that one might ask whether there was actually any difference at all between them. It was apparent that a segment of the profession felt that there was something essentially inadequate about the standard version of the syntactic component, and that limitations should be set on it.[6]

Like other competing theories within the transformational-generative approach, generative semantics was intended to provide a model of the native speaker's competence, but in doing so it sought formally to characterize assumed direct relations between semantic content and speech sounds. There was no constituent structure component in the manner of Chomsky (1965), nor any qualitative difference between semantic representation and syntactic representation. It was explicitly recognized that setting up separate syntactic and semantic components, if at all feasible, involved unnecessary redundancy, since units and categories used in the semantic representation also appeared in the syntactic representation.

These developments created conditions for questioning the need for a sharp differentiation between deep and surface structures. Would it not be more effective to conceive linguistic analysis in terms of a continuum stretching from an area of semantic structures to an area of phonological representations? The treatment passive sentences have received under different frameworks (which is reviewed in the following section) illustrates some of the effects which changes in linguistic theory have had on linguistic description. The analysis presented in this study incorporates some of the findings made possible by modern theories and attempts to characterize the semantic structure of passive sentences, as opposed to that of nonpassive ones; it also tries to show how, in a certain number of cases at least, those differences are reflected in the organization of the surface representation of sentences.

The semantic structure of a sentence being thus considered the starting point of the analysis, the next step is the characterization of the processes which lead to the overt expression of the semantic material. As to the linguistic significance of passives as opposed to nonpassives, this analysis is based to a large extent on notions developed by members of the Prague

School of linguistics, which will be mentioned in more detail further on. First and foremost there is the concept of communicative dynamism (CD), according to which the divers elements of a sentence contribute, in different degrees, to the act of communication. A contrastive analysis of Portuguese and English patterns is provided as an application of the theoretical approach adopted, and some suggestions are made concerning the teaching of Portuguese passives to native speakers of English. The examples used here are either my own or have been culled from tape-recorded conversations or printed sources. In all cases, they were submitted to native speakers of American English or Brazilian Portuguese who served as informants.

This study is a revised version of my Cornell University doctoral thesis (Azevedo 1973), written under the thoughtful guidance of Frederick B. Agard, to whom this edition is gratefully dedicated. It goes without saying that neither Professor Agard nor the other members of my doctoral committee--James S. Noblitt and Gerald B. Kelley, whose assistance is hereby acknowledged--are in any way responsible for whatever errors are still extant. I also thank Father Richard J. O'Brien, S.J., for having encouraged me to prepare this revision for Georgetown University Press, and the University of California, Berkeley, for a summer grant which made it possible to carry out this project.

NOTES

1. See, for example, Wells (1947), Gleason (1955, 1961), Hockett (1958). Tagmemic analysis, however, adopted a somewhat different approach (see Longacre 1960, Elson and Pickett 1968).
2. See also Harris (1951), especially Chapters One and Two.
3. The following passage is relevant: 'Having determined the syntactic structure of the language, we can study the way in which this syntactic structure is put to use in the actual functioning of the language' (Chomsky 1957:102).
4. This is an instance of the model-oriented character of transformational-generative analysis, which in a sense gives continuance to an approach established in the early days of structural descriptive linguistics in the United States. See Gross (1968).
5. This was indirectly suggested by McCawley (1968b:586), who despite his criticisms of Weinreich's model, gave him recognition for his contribution to later developments.
6. For an account of the development of generative semantics and its relations to the standard theory of interpretive semantics, see Searle (1972).

1

THE SEMANTICS OF PASSIVES

1.1 On the notion of passive. The notion of passive is linked with that of voice, which refers to the means whereby, in the grammar of languages like Latin, a distinction is made between morphologically marked verb forms such as Latin *videor* 'I am seen' vs. *video* 'I see'. Forms of the first type serve (with the exception of deponent verbs) to indicate that the grammatical subject of the verb stands for what, on the semantic level, is interpreted as the receiver of an action denoted by the verb; from this contrast stem the idea that in such cases the subject has a somewhat passive role, and the traditional distinction between passive and active sentences.

As adopted in the description of modern languages such as the Romance languages or English, however, the label 'passive' does not refer to verb forms morphologically distinguishable from active ones, but rather to specific syntactic constructions, as in (1b) and (1d).[1]

(1a) Nelson stole the purse.
(1b) The purse was stolen by Nelson.
(1c) Nelson roubou a bolsa.
(1d) A bolsa foi roubada por Nelson.

The distinction between the grammatical subject as a semantic actor, as in (1a) and (1c), or as a semantic patient, as in (1b) and (1d), is linked to those syntactic differences. It also provides the basis for the traditional classification as passives of sentences with the indeterminate pronoun *se* which are analyzed in Chapter Two. While 'passive' may be a useful label, it is also true that any label is only good as long as it designates similar objects. That this label has at times been stretched a little too thin is evidenced by its use in an article on Spanish which

> loosely interprets 'passive' to mean those grammatical structures which either tend to obscure the identity of the subject or which place him in the position of object while making a non-human entity the subject of the sentence. An example of the former would be *se puede*; of the latter *se me murió (mi perro)* (Seelye 1966:290).

It is understandable that the active vs. passive dichotomy should lose some of its clarity if 'passive sentence', as a category, is rendered so vague as to encompass a large number of constructions whose mutual relationships are not readily apparent and sometimes hard to justify on formal grounds. Consequently, it is not surprising that some authors have questioned the validity--or at any rate the usefulness--of that distinction. McKerrow (1922:163), for example, questions the distinction between active and passive voice in modern spoken English and states that 'without knowledge of or reference to the classics, it might never occur to us to postulate a passive voice at all'.

Nevertheless, it would be wasteful to ignore a distinction on which a considerable body of linguistic work is based. The labels 'passive' and 'nonpassive' are useful for identifying the structures exemplified in sentences (1a)-(1d), and provided that we make clear what they refer to, they can serve our purposes fairly adequately. The first step, then, is to clarify what we mean when we talk about passive constructions.

As Svartvik (1966:3) points out, 'there is no agreement among grammarians as to what constitutes an English passive', and one might add that the situation is not much different as regards Portuguese. In his study, Svartvik uses 'passive' to refer to what might be labelled, as he acknowledges in a footnote, occurrences of 'the $\underline{be + V_{ed}}$- construction'. The present study is concerned with a narrower range of constructions, which must be characterized at different levels. As a first approximation, we can say that, at the level of syntactic organization, a passive is characterized by the formula

(2) $NP_1 + VP_{pas} + \text{PrepAgt } NP_2$

which defines a well-formed string in which $NP_1 \neq NP_2$, PrepAgt is a specific preposition,[2] and VP_{pas} is a symbol which can be broken down into AuxPas + Vpart, in which Vpart stands for a past participle of the main verb, and AuxPas is an auxiliary element actualized by a form of *ser* in Portuguese and one of *be* in English.[3]

Grammatically, NP_1 is the subject of VP_{pas} and NP_2 is its agent. Since an indirect object may also be present, structure (2) can be expanded into (3), which includes symbols for these components and their functions. The last parentheses in (3) indicate that there can be passives without the component PrepAgt + NP_2, but they do not imply that every passive can dispense with it.

(3) NP_1:SJ + AuxPas Vpart + (NP_3:IO) + (PrepAgt NP_2:Agt)

This narrowing of our subject matter has the effect of excluding from consideration sentences containing the so-called active verbs with passive meaning (Almeida 1967, Erades 1950), as well as, for the time being, at least, sentences like (4), which are sometimes called 'stative passives' (Ptg. 'passivas de estado').

(4) A porta já estava fechada quando chegamos lá.
'The door was already closed when we got there.'

It is possible to establish three types of distinctions between the passives and their nonpassive counterparts of (1). To begin with, there are the syntactical relationships: *Nelson*, the subject in (1a), (1c), appears in (1b), (1d) as the surface agent. Then there are the semantic relations between the referentials denoted by the different lexical items: in either sentence, the same noun plays the same semantic role, i.e. *Nelson* does the stealing and *the purse* = *a bolsa* gets stolen in either case. The third type of relationship is perhaps less evident, since those sentences are not placed in any context. For the moment, it will suffice to say that these relationships have to do with the fact that, while in (1a), (1c) something is predicated about *Nelson*, in (1b), (1d) something else is predicated about *the purse* = *a bolsa*.

These three types of relationships can be analyzed as belonging to three separate but closely interrelated levels,[4] which are schematically shown in Table 1. The advantage of this approach is that it enables us to isolate and relate three components of any instance of communication: (a) the actual content of the message, that is, its semantic elements and their internal structuring; (b) the arrangement of those elements into a rule-governed structure provided by the syntax; and (c) their distribution in the surface structure of the sentence, according to their respective informative value. As regards the latter, any message must be placed within a context and structured in function of certain presuppositions and postsuppositions which the speaker-writer makes about what he wants to communicate. The ideal description of a linguistic system should provide, for an analysis of a given sentence, a description of the elements at work at each one of those levels. Moreover, it should indicate the relevant interlevel relationships, that is, how elements of the different levels fit together (in the sense of accord with one another) in the message.

In considering the relations between passives and nonpassives, then, we have to do with three orders of formal objects. At the grammatical (surface or syntactical) level, with 'functions' such as subject, direct and indirect object, and agent; at the semantic level, with 'categories' such as actor, goal, and beneficiary; and at the level of distribution of information, with the

Table 1. Levels of sentence structure.

	Prague School[a]	M. A. K. Halliday[b]	W. Chafe[c]
Syntactical relations	Level of grammatical structure: categories like subject, object, etc., based on syntactic form rather than on semantic content, and which are the 'bearers of a linguistic function in the given system'.	Level of interpersonal function: distinctions of mood and modality; characterization of 'grammatical subjects' as opposed to 'logical subjects' or 'actors' and of 'grammatical objects' as opposed to 'goals' and 'beneficiaries'.	Level of sentence organization in terms of surface functions like 'subject', 'object', etc.
Semantic relations	Level of semantic structure: it contains 'the linguistic relevant generalizations of concrete lexical meanings that enter the semantic structure of the sentence', formulated as 'abstract word categories (e.g. living being, individual, quality, action) or of relations between these categories (e.g. action as feature of an individual)'; 'relations such as actor and action; bearer of a quality or of a state and the state; action and the object resulting from the action or touched by it ...circumstances of place, time; relations of cause and consequence, etc.'	Ideational function: structuring of experience into participant functions of 'actor', 'goal', and 'beneficiary', as well as 'transitivity roles' of process, 'participant', 'circumstance'.	Organization of semantic bundles in terms of selectional and inflectional units such as verb, noun, animate, action, state, process, etc. Establishment of semantic functions such as agent, beneficiary, patient, complement. Establishment of semantic relationships between semantic bundles in terms of those functions.
Relationships of distribution of information	Level of organization of utterance: how the information contained in the semantic level is organized into theme-transition-rheme, by means of syntactic categories and taking into account the 'linear materialization and linear perception of utterance...[and] the extralinguistic content of the message...the context and situation and...the attitude of the speaker towards the message and the addressee'.	Structuring of the message into theme ('psychological subject') and rheme. Organization of information structure in terms of 'given' and 'new'.	Distribution of old and new information in the semantic structure.

a. Cf. Daneš (1966).
b. Cf. Halliday (1970).
c. Cf. Chafe (1970).

organization of sentence elements into a structure of 'theme' and 'rheme'. More will be said in due time about the notions expressed by these terms. Before that, I am going to review the treatment of passives by different authors.

1.2 A note on background. The study of passives has often been conceived as the analysis of the relationships between their semantic and syntactic characteristics and the corresponding features of their active counterparts. This is the approach usually found in many of the so-called traditional grammars, where it is often assumed that a passive and its nonpassive counterpart have the same meaning. For example, Palmer (1965:62) states that there are no differences in meaning between passives and actives other than the 'formal feature that the object of the active verb is the subject of the passive while the subject of the active is the "agent" of the passive'. Joos (1968:95) characterizes the passive as a word-order device, and states that 'the meaning of the passive is that the subject does not designate the actor. This is in fact all that can be said about the meaning...The subject designates some entity which is intimately involved in the event...' Some authors, however, have indicated that there are meaning differences between such pairs of sentences. Sweet (1898:113), for example, characterizes the passive voice as a 'grammatical device', one of the functions of which consists in 'bringing the object of a transitive verb into prominence by making it the subject of the sentence'. Further on, I discuss what is meant by saying that the subject position is one of prominence in English (or in Portuguese, for that matter); but we may notice for now that 'prominence' is a notion which has to do with the semantics of an utterance, since it is part and parcel of what the speaker wants to communicate. More or less in the same vein, Jespersen (1948:120) states that, although an active sentence and its passive counterpart

> mean essentially the same thing...they are not in every respect synonymous...as a rule the person or thing that is at the centre of interest at the moment is made the subject of the sentence, and therefore the verb is in some cases put in the active, in others in the passive.

Some traditional authors have interpreted the formation of passives as the result of an unformalized transformation[5] which, operating on active sentences such as *Nelson killed Milton* = *Nelson matou Milton*, has the effect of (a) moving the direct object to the subject slot; (b) inserting the adequate AuxPas; (c) replacing the original verbal form with the past participle; and (d) rewriting the original subject as an agentive element preceded by a specific preposition after the AuxPas + Vpart construction. Without such unformalized transformations, neither traditional nor structuralist grammars would be able to account for the relationships between actives and passives. As Searle (1972:18) puts it:

> Phrase structure rules were...already implicit in at least some of the structuralist grammars...For example, in spite of the different word order and the addition of certain elements, the sentence 'The book will be read by the boy' and the sentence 'The boy will read the book' have much in common; they both mean the same thing--the only difference is that one is in the passive mood and the other in the active mood. Phrase structure grammars alone give us no way to picture this similarity. They would give us two unrelated descriptions of these two sentences.

Other authors have not insisted on the active-to-passive direction of derivation. Jespersen himself (1948) mentions only the possibility of conveying the same idea in two ways, but he does not assign priority to either the active or the passive. Likewise, Zandwoort (1960:53) describes the English passive voice as 'a verbal group consisting of one of the forms of *to be* plus the past participle of a transitive verb', without going into the question of whether such a verbal group necessarily derives from an active construction.

The question of the formation of passives depends in great part on what is contained in their semantic structures that is not included in the semantic make-up of nonpassive counterparts. As to what such differences may consist of, a number of authors have restated, with minor variations, the views put forth by Jespersen. Charleston (1960:286-287), for example, incorporates Jespersen's comments almost literally, adding that

> the active form sees an agent 'doing something' to another being or object. The passive form sees the being or thing 'suffering' some activity at the hands of the agent...When the active form is chosen, prominence is given to the agent. When the passive form is used, the 'sufferer' is given prominence as subject of the passive construction. The choice of the active or the passive voice is therefore subjective.

Mihailović (1963:78) puts forth a different view, according to which, at least 'in passive utterances where the author is suppressed', the shift of the active object to subject position cannot be regarded as a device for giving prominence to the active object, since in a subject + predicate language such as English 'the initial position of the subject does not make it particularly prominent'. It is important, according to that author, to make a distinction between passives 'in which the subject is suppressed and [passives]...in which it is transformed into an adverbial adjunct', since choice between these two constructions is not 'a matter of vague personal preference' and 'the use of the two constructions is not determined by the same factors'. The use of a passive without an agent phrase would be determined by the 'need to get rid of a subject which adds no significant information to the sentence and a desire for objectivity of attitude'. The *by* + Agt construction, on the other hand, would be 'a device for giving prominence to the subject of the active verb. When the actor is shifted to final position, primary stress falls on it, and makes it very prominent'.

Hill (1963:73), however, rejects both Sweet's and Mihailović's views, arguing that 'it is possible to make either the front position or the end position the most emphatic, and..both the active and the passive are found with both of these alternatives'. Relative prominence of either the active subject or the active object would not be the determinant factor in the choice between the two constructions.

The notion of passives as transforms of active sentences, implicitly or explicitly contained in a number of traditional studies, was adopted by many linguists working with the transformational-generative framework. A fundamental difference between the two approaches, however, is that they do not concern themselves with the same sort of formal objects. Traditional grammars study surface sentences, or the representation of utterances in orthography or speech, whereas transformational-generative analysis operates on abstract constructs, such as phrase-markers generated through the application of phrase-structure rules and transformations, which are related to, but not identical with, the constituents of surface sentences. Thus, Chomsky (1957:112) describes passives as deriving, not from surface active sentences, but rather from the terminal of a (by definition active) kernel sentence which meets the structural description shown in (5), through the application of an optional transformation, Tpas (6), which transposes the two NPs, adds *by* before the second NP, and adds *be + en* to the auxiliary constituent.

(5) NP - Aux - V - NP

(6) Tpas: $X_1 - X_2 - X_3 - X_4 \rightarrow X_4 - X_2 + \text{be} + \text{en} - X_3 - \text{by} + X_1$

The possibility of applying Tpas depends on the presence of a transitive verb in the kernel sentence. Chomsky (1957:79f.) justified this analysis, which assigns to passives the character of derived sentences, on grounds of formal simplicity, for otherwise the inclusion of passives among the kernel sentences would complicate the phrase structure rules considerably.

That formulation, however, left a few questions pending. For example, as Chomsky himself noted (1957:100-101), in certain sentences involving quantifiers, such as his own examples in (7), the relations between passives and actives are ambiguous.

(7a) Everyone in the room knows two languages.
(7b) Two languages are known by everyone in the room.

Besides, not all transitive verbs can undergo passivization, as Lees (1960:8) remarked about the so-called 'middle verbs' such as *resemble, look like, cost, weigh, mean*, etc., whose presence in a kernel sentence would block the application of Tpas--a fact which accounts for the ungrammaticality of the sentences of (9), supposedly derived from the kernel sentences of (8). As evidenced by the Portuguese examples in both sets, the application of Chomsky's theory (1957) to this language would encounter similar difficulties.

(8a) The movie cost eight million dollars.
(8a') O filme custou oito milhões de cruzeiros.
(8b) John weighs one hundred and fifty pounds.
(8b') João pesa setenta e cinco quilos.
(8c) Peter looks like a clown.
(8c') Pedro parece um palhaço.

(9a) *Eight million dollars were cost by the movie.
(9a') *Oito milhões de dólares foram custados pelo filme.
(9b) *One hundred and fifty pounds are weighed by John.
(9b') *Setenta e cinco quilos são pesados por João.
(9c) *A clown is looked like by Peter.
(9c') *Um palhaço é parecido por Pedro.

The introduction of the constituents *by* + X_1 and *be* + *en* also posed certain theoretical problems regarding the basis and goals of TG. Lees remarked that the presence of those elements on the right side of rule (6) made it 'a-typical of grammatical transformations in general' and did not 'provide for the correct constituent structure of the resulting passive sentences' (Lees 1964, cited in Svartvik 1966:2). Lees proposed (1960:34) that the *be* + *en* element should be included in the Auxiliary; as to *by* + X_1, he suggested (1964:29-30, cited in Svartvik 1966:2) that any sentence with a transitive verb might also have an agentive constituent. If the latter were realized in the surface structure, the result would be a passive sentence; if not, an active sentence would be generated.[6]

An improved analysis was presented by Katz and Postal (1964), who questioned the view that passives and actives are transformationally related, while maintaining that an active sentence and its passive counterpart are paraphrases of each other. In their formulation (1964:72), a passive derives from an underlying phrase-marker 'containing an Adverb manner constituent dominating *by* plus a passive morpheme dummy'. That constituent would be one of the possible realizations of $\text{Adverb}_{\text{manner}}$; once present in the phrase-marker, however, it would obligatorily determine the application of the passive transformation.

This analysis was accepted by Chomsky (1965:104ff.), thus replacing his previous formulation, over which it had several advantages. By restricting passivization to verbs which can take manner adverbials freely, the new rules accounted not only for passive sentences with transitive verbs, such as *kill*, *kiss*, etc., but also for passive constructions involving intransitive verbs (e.g. *John is looked up to by everyone*, Chomsky 1965: 104). They also eliminated the problem raised by Lees' 'middle verbs', since these may not take manner adverbials.[7] Also, sentence pairs like those in (7) were disambiguated by means of an analysis which showed that 'actives and passives containing quantifiers and pronouns are ambiguous in the same way and so are full paraphrases of each other' (Katz and Postal 1964:72). This view, challenged by Ziff (1966), was reasserted by Katz and Martin (1967), who argued that Ziff's criticism only held good when applied to the establishment of paraphrase relations between those sentences at the surface level. Since the objects of Katz and Postal's analysis were 'not sentences but certain abstract syntactic structures underlying them, which at first approximation may be thought of as corresponding to syntactically unambiguous sentences' (Katz and Martin 1967: 478), that analysis could not, it was argued, be disproved by Ziff's arguments.

Another obstacle to the view that passives and actives are paraphrases of each other was apparently inherent in the fact that, in the new formulation, different phrase-markers were required for the generation of an active sentence and its corresponding passive. However, as pointed out by Goldin (1968: 23ff.), the Katz-Postal-Chomsky approach sidestepped this difficulty by assigning to passive the status of a dummy constituent which did not receive a semantic interpretation. The following passage is revealing.

> ...sentences with the same underlying phrase marker or underlying phrase markers that are the same, except for elements that do not bear meaning, are marked as--predicted to be--synonymous by the grammar. It is just for this reason that the claim about the synonymy of actives and passives was formulated as the thesis that an active *underlying phrase marker* and its corresponding passive *underlying phrase marker* receive the same semantic interpretation (Katz and Martin 1967: 480).

The split undergone by generative-transformational analysis in the mid-sixties yielded several theoretical proposals concerning language analysis. One of these, Fillmore's (1968) case grammar, characterizes passivization as the result of the choice of a 'nonnormal' surface subject. Given an underlying configuration such as that of (10), the verb (V) is obligatorily specified as [+ passive] if a constituent other than the Agentive (A) --such as the Objective (O) or the Dative (D)--is chosen for direct insertion under the symbol S.

(10a)

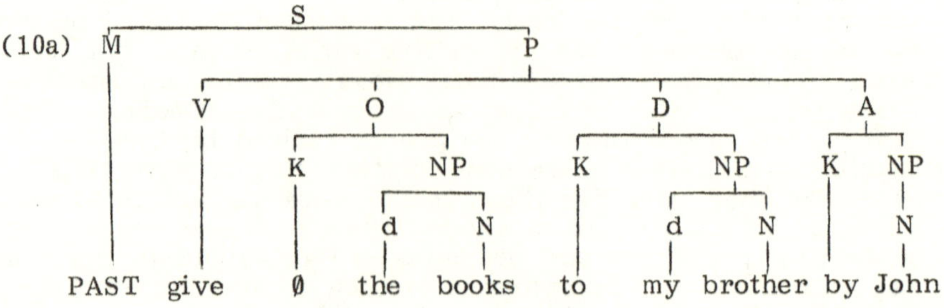

(10b) Agentive chosen as subject

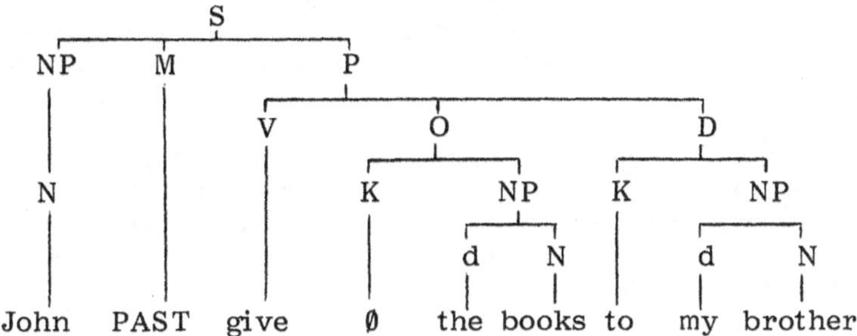

(10c) Objective chosen as subject

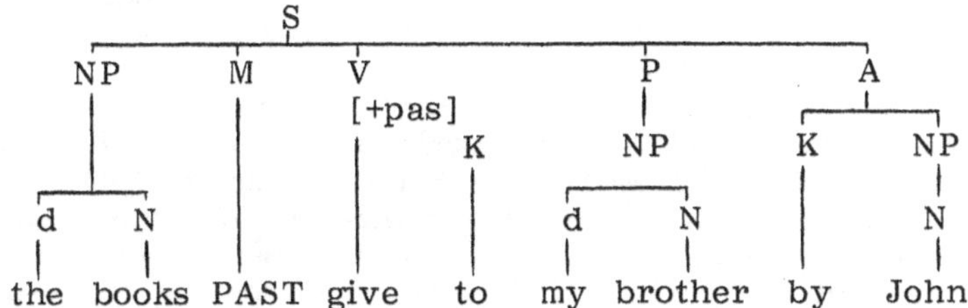

(10d) Dative chosen as subject

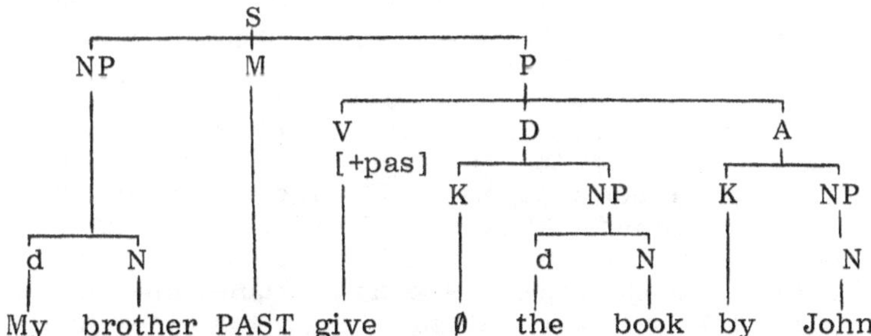

Case grammar avoids the controversy of whether passives derive from (surface or underlying) active sentences or have an independent formation, by postulating the same underlying structure for both passives and actives. However, although case grammar emphasizes that the semantic relations among different constituents remain unaltered whether the sentence is ultimately actualized as a passive or as a nonpassive, it does not provide a motivation for the choice of one constituent over another for subjectivization. That is, it does not clarify what would lead a speaker to choose a 'nonnormal' subject, and it implies an equivalence between passives and their nonpassive counterparts.

As to the use of passives, several authors have provided answers involving the relative prominence of the NPs concerned

(Jespersen, Sweet, Mihailović, Hill), but there is some divergence among them as to the interpretations of the constructions involved. Analyzers of Portuguese have not given much attention to this matter; an exception is Thomas (1969:195), who states that

> by shifting the use of a noun or a pronoun from object to subject, a shift in sentence order is made natural. The performer of the act, which is the logical subject, now becomes the agent and comes last in the sentence--a more emphatic position...

However, Thomas does not indicate why that position is to be considered more emphatic than others. There are also authors who either sidestep the problem (Palmer, Joos), or take a stand for the semantic equivalence of actives and passives (Katz, Postal, Martin, Chomsky).

It seems that insistence on the semantic equivalence of passives and nonpassives should be ascribed to the fact that the theoretical frameworks used by these authors do not include relations obtaining at the level of organization of information (cf. Table 1). By concentrating on isolated sentences, they can only account for part of the semantic content of those sentences, that is, for their cognitive meaning. As far as this is concerned, it is correct to state that, say, *Peter killed the boar* means the same (i.e. has the same truth value) as *The boar was killed by Peter.* But for the analysis to go beyond the structure of isolated sentences, it must account for the different ways in which the same cognitive content can be organized to answer different needs of discourse structure.

The answers to the related question of the formation of passives fall into two major categories. On the one hand, there are those that propound a derivation based on either surface structures (Pereira n.d.) or underlying kernel sentences (Chomsky 1957). Most authors who have studied the problem in Portuguese belong to this category.[8] On the other hand, there is the view that passives and nonpassives are generated independently, either from the same deep structure (Fillmore 1968) or from very similar deep structures (Katz and Postal 1964, Chomsky 1965, Katz and Martin 1967). There are also authors who limit themselves to stating the relationships between passives and actives (Jespersen, Sweet, Zandvoort), without committing themselves to the view that passives are formally derived from active sentences.

1.3 Theoretical considerations. In the theory of meaning developed by Chafe,[9] for whom language is a symbolic device for representing experience by means of speech sounds, relationships between content and expression are basic. According to this view, the content of experience is initially organized in semantic configurations, and the initial stage of symbolization consists in the arrangement of semantic features or units into sets, the elements of which are incorporated in order of decreasing generality and increasing specificity.

Semantic configurations include two main types of elements: (a) predicative elements or semantic verbs, which have to do with 'states (conditions, qualities) and events' and (b) nominal elements or semantic nouns, which have to do 'with "things" (both physical objects and reified abstractions)' (Chafe 1970: 96). The nucleus of a sentence is typically a verb, the specification of which determines the presence and the semantic characteristics of accompanying nouns. Thus, verbs are supposed to have a certain precedence over cooccurring nouns and to provide a certain orientation for the generation of sentences.

A semantic verb (symbolized V) is initially specified by 'selectional units', such as state, which creates a general division between state and nonstate verbs; the latter can be specified for features like action, process, ambient, experiential, benefactive, and so on. The process of specification takes place by means of rules like those of (11).[10]

(11a) V ——▷▷ state
(11b) V_{-state} ——▷▷ process
action

Nouns are also specified by selectional rules, such as those of (12).

(12a) N ——▷▷ count
potent
(12b) [count potent] ——▷▷ animate

Selectional units are introduced in a hierarchical fashion, each unit being more specific than the one immediately preceding, thus narrowing the semantic specification of a V or N and setting limits on the choice of a maximally specific lexical unit, represented by a verb or noun root (underlined in the examples), the insertion of which signals the end of this phase. The formulae of (13) exemplify the rules which introduce lexical units.

(13a) [state -ambient] ▷▷dry, tight [e.g. The clothes are dry.] ,
(13b) [process -action] ▷▷dry, tighten [e.g. The clothes dried.]
(13c) [process action] ▷▷dry, tighten, break [e.g. Mary dried the clothes.]

The result of the application of a series of selectional rules, followed by the insertion of a lexical unit, is the partial semantic configuration of a verb or noun, as represented in (14).

(14) V state dry | V process die | V action sing | V action process kill

(14)	V	V	V	V
	state	process	action	action
	dry	die	sing	process
				kill

Noun and verb roots can be further specified for other semantic features, represented by inflectional units, which 'do not influence the choice of lexical units...[and] typically, though not always,...have some overt surface representation' (Chafe 1970: 168). Among inflectional units for verbs we can cite, for example, generic, past, future, perfective, and progressive. Units for nouns include, among others, generic, definite, aggregate, and plural. These units are introduced by rules like those of (15).

(15a) V
-state
experiential
benefactive
—— ——▷▷ generic

(15b) V —— ——▷▷ past
(15c) V —— ——▷▷ future

The selectional units of a verb 'determine the number and relation of accompanying nouns' (Chafe 1970: 114). For example, action-process verbs such as *kill* and *murder* require an actor noun root which is animate and therefore specified also as count and potent; *murder*, on the other hand, would require a human goal since one usually speaks of either murdering or killing human beings, but only of killing animals. The formation of structures made up of a verb and one or more nouns is described by replacement rules[11] of the type shown in (16). For example, a configuration represented by a state or process verb is obligatorily replaced by one which includes, besides the original verb, a patient noun root as in (16a). Likewise, an action verb must be replaced by a configuration which contains, besides that verb, an agent noun root, as in (16b). Both of these rules apply to action-process verbs, yielding a configuration such as that in (16c).

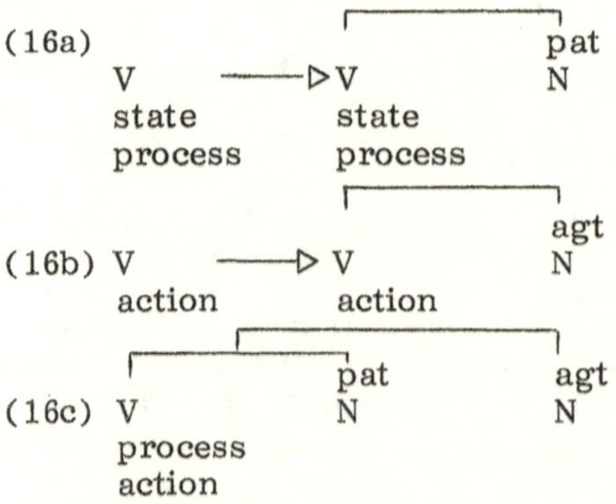

After the elements of a semantic configuration have been characterized and the relations among them established, the resulting configuration undergoes a series of postsemantic processes,[12] each of which yields an intermediate postsemantic structure. The latter is converted into an underlying phonological representation by a process of symbolization (Chafe 1970: 234). There follow certain phonological processes which ultimately provide a phonetic representation of the sentence. In this study, however, I am not concerned with postsemantic processes beyond the establishment of surface structures, except by way of reference to certain phonological phenomena of stress and pitch which are relevant for the study of passive sentences.

Let us consider the simplified semantic configuration of the sentence *The boys will sing the Messiah.*

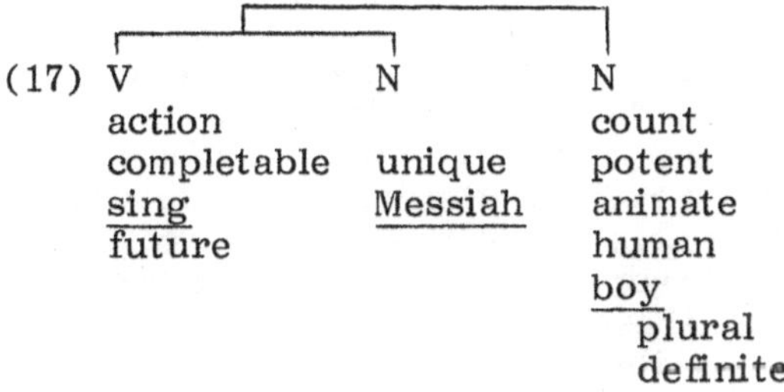

Among the postsemantic processes that generate a surface structure from (17), there are the following.

1.3.1 Surface function assignment. Since semantic relations like agent and patient appear in the surface structure as subjects (SJ) and objects (DO and IO), there must be a set of rules determining which such function is occupied by each noun root. Let us assume that if the agent noun is chosen as subject in (17), this choice determines that the patient noun is assigned the function of direct object.

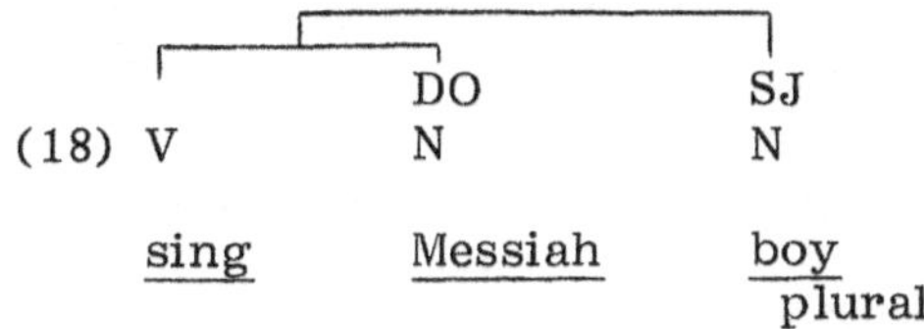

1.3.2 Literalization. This includes processes which convert certain semantic units into 'arbitrary configurations of postsemantic units before a surface structure is reached' (Chafe 1970: 246). For example, the unit future must be represented by a surface auxiliary verb introduced by a rule like (19), which gives rise to (20).

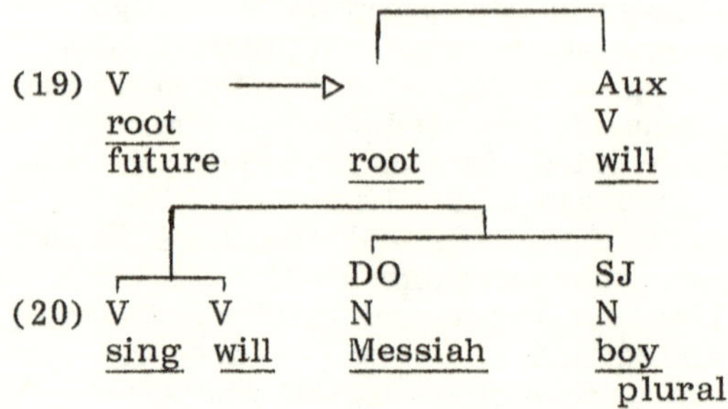

1.3.3 **Primary linearization (PL) rules.** These establish the relative position of the elements in the configuration. Rule (21) places the auxiliary verb before the main verb root; rule (22) places the subject before the group formed by the two verbs; and rule (23) places the direct object after its verb. Once the position of an element has been determined, labels like Aux, SJ, etc., are deleted as redundant. Selectional units, which also become redundant after the choice of a lexical unit, are deleted by rules of the general type (24), where X represents 'whatever units are positioned in a semantic structure diagram between the V or N and the root' (Chafe 1970:255). After all these rules have applied, there is a semantic configuration of the type (25).

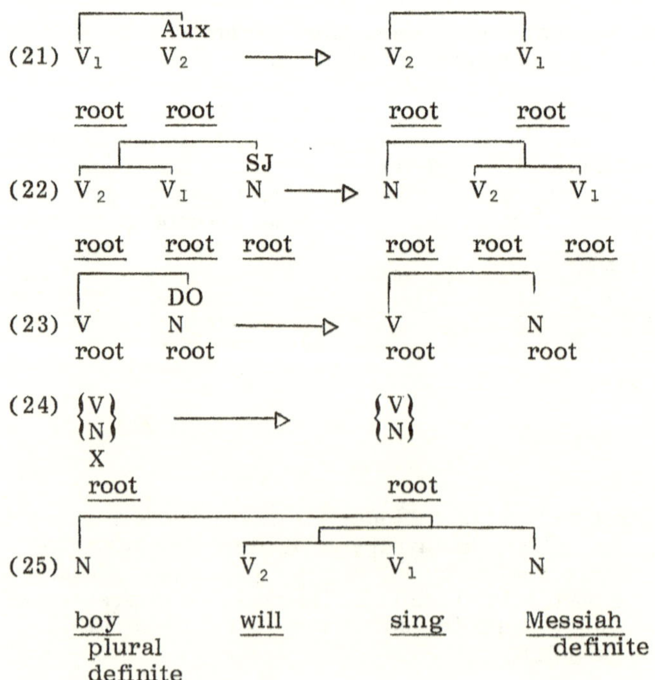

1.3.4 Secondary linearization (SL) rules. These rules take care of the ordering of semantic units within each element. Rules like those of (26) seem to be relevant in this case.

(26a) N definite ——▷ definite N

(26b) N plural ——▷ N plural

In (26a), '*definite* is linearized to precede the noun, to become, at this stage, the item which we would identify traditionally as the definite article' (Chafe 1970:256). Likewise, in (26b) plural is eventually identified with the plural morpheme, represented by S in (27b). Eventually, these two units are replaced by surface structure elements, as in (27). After all secondary linearization rules have applied, a configuration like that of (28) results, ready to go through a process of symbolization, the result of which will be an 'input to the phonological rules of English' (Chafe 1970:257).

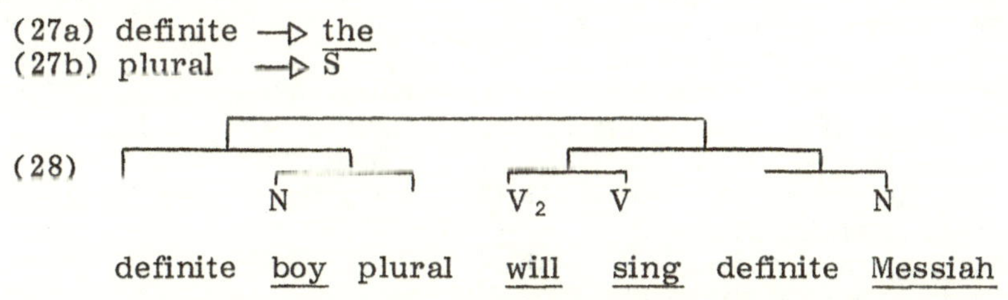

This approach is generative (Bolinger 1961:381), in the sense that it accounts for processes of sentence formation. Furthermore, it has some points in common with generative semantics, in that it does not set up either totally separate components, or qualitative differences between semantic and syntactic phenomena. However, the two approaches diverge in their interpretation of what constitutes the semantic content of a sentence. Generative semantics is concerned mainly with the cognitive content of sentences, and it generally accepts that semantic representation (= cognitive meaning) can be adequately described in terms of symbolic logic. Thus, just as certain categories of symbolic logic can be reduced to others, it would also be feasible to reduce the number of categories necessary for semantic representation to a small number, which would match 'in almost one-to-one fashion the categories of symbolic logic' (McCawley 1970:169; see also McCawley 1969:Section 4).

Chafe's model, however, takes into account the broader significance which sentences have as bearers of messages, and thus it goes beyond cognitive content alone. Excessive preoccupation with the latter may result in what Chafe calls the 'X is really Y syndrome', which consists in analyzing different surface sentences--such as, say, those of (29) and (30)--as different surface manifestations of the same deep semantic structure.

(29) Peter killed his son.
(30) Peter's son was killed by his father.

Assuming that the nouns in each sentence have the same referents, and that in each case the possessive refers to the subject (rather than to someone else), it can be said that, from a logical standpoint, if one of these sentences is true (or false), the other is also true (or false). The criterion of truth value (or identity of cognitive content), however,

> is misleading, and the only valid criterion for sameness of meaning must be whether one surface structure conveys exactly the same message, thoughts, concepts, or ideas as another (Chafe 1970:87-88).

But in order to grasp the full significance of a sentence as a message, one must take into account that in ordinary language use sentences do not occur in a contextual vacuum, but rather are uttered for purposes of communication against a background of information which can be created verbally and/or established on the basis of shared information. Somehow, the background should be taken into account in the semantic description, since it serves to establish constraints on the organization of the cognitive meaning proper.

Insofar as our research has shown, Chafe has been the first author to try to incorporate formally the concepts of shared and unshared information into a generative model of language description. From the viewpoint of the analysis of existing sentences, in a surface-to-semantic-structure approach, as it were,[13] several linguists have made important contributions to the clarification of those concepts and their role in communication.[14]

A passive verb is always related to at least one noun root. For example, if the verb is specified for action (31a) or action-process (31b), that noun will be a patient; an action-process-completive verb[15] will be associated with a complement noun, as in (31c); an action-process verb which is also marked as benefactive may be associated with both a patient and a beneficiary noun (31d). In all of these cases, an agent noun may be present as well. If an action-process verb is marked as experiential, the surface agent will correspond to an experiencer in the semantic structure (31e).

(31a) Peter was shouted at by one of the secretaries.
(31b) The dog was killed by a cop.

(31c) The castle was built in a year by the slaves.
(31d) The book was given to Paul by the rector.
(31e) John was seen at the dance by his girl friend.

The distinctions between patient and complement, agent and experiencer, etc., are very useful for analyzing the different semantic contents of the nouns in a given semantic configuration. However, as Halliday (1970:147) points out, although such distinctions

> account for systematic distinctions in the grammar...there may be many, often contradictory criteria to choose from... the more categories one sets up, the more indeterminate instances will arise...

The discussion of the semantic functions of nouns can be simplified by grouping different semantic distinctions under the same label, which will refer, in turn, to what Halliday calls 'participant functions' of the noun. Thus, patient and complement nouns are referred to as goals and experiencer, and agent nouns as actors; the label beneficiary indicates a participant function which can be filled by a variety of semantic concepts, such as 'recipient of an object' (as in *Peter was given a book*), 'recipient of a service' (as in *The house was painted for Peter*), 'recipient of a command' (as in *Peter was ordered to leave*), and so forth (Halliday 1970:Section 3).

This terminology has the advantage of establishing a fixed set of functional relationships at the level of semantic configurations, while at the same time freeing the analyst to introduce further refinements in the classification of the semantic roles of the nouns. It also implies a methodological change which consists in attributing to the notions of agent, experiencer, complement, and the like, the character of selectional features of nouns. That is, nouns are specified as actors, goals, and beneficiaries as regards their participant function. In addition, an actor noun, for instance, is selectionally specified as either agent, or experiencer, etc., depending on its role as regards the semantic specification of the associated verb or verbs. Table 2 summarizes this classification.

Of special importance for the analysis of passives in Chafe's theory is the notion of old vs. new information. The former is constituted by whatever the speaker and the hearer share and which provides 'a kind of starting point based on concepts already "in the air" to which new information can be related' (Chafe 1970:211). Some of this can be part of what the interlocutors know about themselves and the world around them, and some of it may be created verbally. Newness of information is indicated by the inflectional unit 'new', which affects, rather than 'a whole verb or noun, a particular semantic unit within a verb or noun' (Chafe 1970:212). A noun or verb root unspecified for that unit implicitly represents old information.[16] Furthermore, newness of information

> is reflected in English surface structures in two ways: through the establishment of surface structure *subjects* and through intonation. In what may be called the 'least marked' instances, a surface structure subject carries the old information of a sentence...Surface structure items which reflect *new* information are (with some exceptions) spoken with a higher pitch...than those which reflect old information, as might be expected from the fact that it is primarily the new information the speaker wants to convey (Chafe 1970:212-213).

Table 2. Participant functions and semantic roles.

Participant functions	Semantic roles (defined by selectional features)
actor	agent experiencer . . . . . .
goal	patient complement . . . . . .
beneficiary	recipient of { an object a favor a command . . . . . .

In the case of the least marked distribution of new, then, the intonation of a sentence like (32b) reflects, through the presence of high-falling pitch on *fox*, that this goal noun root carries new information, as opposed to the noun *David*. As indicated in (32c), this latter noun can be pronominalized, a possibility normally available to nonnew lexical units (Chafe 1970:223). On the other hand, since the subject position in English usually is not marked by high pitch, it normally contains nouns which are not new. Sometimes, however, 'the patient noun root of an action-process verb conveys old information and...the agent noun root conveys new information' (Chafe 1970:219), and in such cases it would not do to have the patient noun root appear in a position which, because of its high pitch, should be reserved for an element specified as new. According to Chafe, English accommodates this situation by means of the selectional unit passive, which has two functions. The first of these consists in changing 'the order or priorities for the distribution of new information' (Chafe 1970:220), so that the patient noun root can carry old information while the actor noun root carries new information and can, therefore, be assigned to a high-pitch position, as in (33).

(32a) What did David do?
(32b) Oh, David killed the ^{3}fox^{1}.
(32c) Oh, he killed the ^{3}fox^{1}.

(33a) What happened to the wolf?
(33b) The wolf was killed by a ^{3}hunter^{1}.
(33c) It was killed by a ^{3}hunter^{1}.

It should be noted that the verb root is specified as new in the least marked case of distribution of this unit. Nonetheless, surface verbs do not always receive a pitch indicative of new information if they are followed by a new noun root, as in (32b), (32c), and (33b), (33c). A verb does receive that pitch, however, if it is followed by a pronominalized nonnew noun, as in (34b), or when in absolute final position, as in (34c).

(34a) What did the hunter do when he saw the beast?
(34b) He ^{3}killed it^{1}.
(34c) He ^{3}screamed^{1}.

The selectional feature passive, when present in the specification of a verb root, triggers a postsemantic transformation (the possible form of which is discussed later on) which creates surface verb phrases such as those of sentences (33b), (33c).
The second function of passive consists in making it possible for 'an action-process or experiential-process verb to exist without an accompanying agent or experiencer' (Chafe 1970:219), as in the sentences of (35).

(35a) The pier was destroyed.
(35b) Maria Callas was heard.

Initially, Chafe tries to make the assignment of a noun root to the function of subject dependent on the distribution of new. For the least marked case of this unit, a rule would cause a nonnew root to become the subject of the verb, as illustrated in the diagrams of (36).

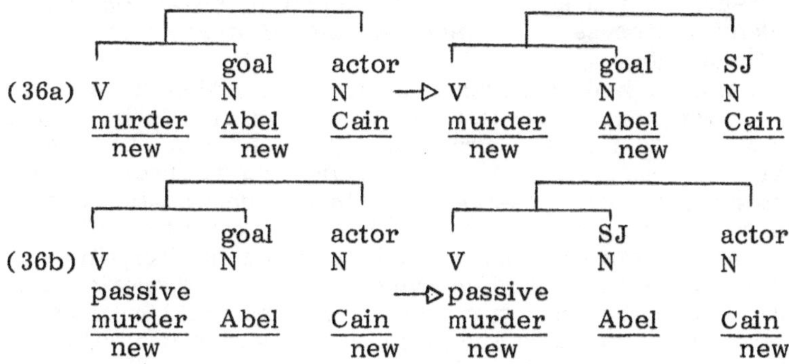

Other distributions of new are possible, however, which preclude the application of the subject-assignment rule as just stated. As Chafe remarks, certain new nouns must become surface subjects, and some nonnew nouns should not become subjects, as in the semantic configuration represented in (37), which generates the sentences of (38), in which the noun root *Fred* becomes the subject in spite of being specified as new. It should be noticed that this noun does not necessarily receive high pitch, as in (38b'), even though it contains new information.[17]

		goal	actor
(37)	V	N	N
		patient	agent
	kiss	Martha	Fred

(38a) What happened?
(38b') ^{2}Fred kissed ^{3}Martha^{1}.
(38b") ^{3}Fred^{2} ^{2}kissed ^{3}Martha^{1}.

A possible way of solving this problem would consist in making the subject assignment rule dependent

> on the distribution of newness which is present, not at the time the rule applies, but at the earlier, least marked stage when such a statement would be correct (Chafe 1970:244).

However, Chafe ultimately decides, 'without any overwhelming conviction that this is the right course', to regard subjects as 'established not directly on the basis of distribution of new and old information, but instead on the basis of the semantic relations agent, patient, and so on' (1970:243).

Chafe's view of passive sentences resembles that of Katz and Postal (1964) in that it characterizes passivization (or rather, the unit passive) as a semantic element which does not receive a semantic interpretation of its own. Rather, this element serves to bring about modifications in the surface structure of sentences, as regards both the presence of otherwise obligatory elements (such as the agent or experiencer of an action-process or experiential-process verb) and the distribution of other units (such as new).

It is debatable, however, whether features which do not receive a semantic interpretation of their own should be included in the semantic part of the grammar. The approach proposed here characterizes passivization as a surface phenomenon and thus allows the feature passive to be introduced postsemantically, as a consequence of, rather than as a condition for, special arrangements of semantic units. By characterizing passivization as a surface phenomenon, the theory may gain in generality, since it is not apparent that a feature like passive should be thought of as enjoying universal semantic status. As will be seen presently, the function Chafe attributed to the unit passive can be fulfilled without recourse to it.

Beginning with the second function, one may inquire why action-process or experiential-process verbs should have to be inflected as passive as a condition for appearing dissociated from an actor noun. Why not say that a semantic structure including such a verb may, but does not necessarily have to, include an actor? In a dialogue such as (39), why should one assume that sentence (39b) has ever contained an actor which was deleted somewhere on the way from the semantic to the surface structure?

(39a) What about your father?
(39b) Oh, he was killed in the war.

It is true that a number of analyses carried out under some of the frameworks mentioned in this survey do characterize agentless passives as deriving from passives with an agent clause, through deletion of the latter. However, this procedure is only defensible in cases in which the surface agent can be recovered from the context. There are a number of cases in which there is no apparent way of recovering an agent, and in such situations grammars usually postulate an underlying dummy actor, often symbolized as *somebody*,[18] which is deleted after passivization has applied. But is it absolutely necessary for the description to postulate that a sentence such as *The window was broken last night* is a transform, through passivization and agent deletion, of another sentence such as DUMMY SUBJECT [i.e. someone, something, etc.] + *broke the window last night*? In a generative approach which precludes the formation of sentences without an actor, by means of an obligatory rule like S → NP + VP, for example, the postulation of such dummy actors may be inevitable, but the question is whether such a rule is necessary in the first place.

A possible justification for the use of a dummy actor would be that the concept of an action-process is indissolubly linked to that of an actor; therefore, the occurrence of an action-process verb in a semantic configuration must be accompanied by the occurrence of an actor noun. However, while one might tentatively agree (there are no bases for settling, one way or the other, arguments based on intuition) that the concept of action-process implies that of an actor, it does not follow that the linguistic expression of an action-process must of necessity be associated with that of an actor. In other words, it is a fact of this world that action-processes are caused by actors--people get killed, kissed, etc., by agents of some sort. In organizing semantic material which includes the description of action-processes, however, a language like English or Portuguese can totally omit any mention of agents, and there is no reason why the semantic configuration of a sentence must include such an agent just for the sake of deleting it afterwards.

The notion that the underlying representation (semantic or syntactic) of a passive sentence must include an actor noun, whether or not the latter is realized in the surface representation, seems to be a residue from a long tradition of describing passives as transforms of actives. However, since recent studies have cast doubt on the adequacy of that position,[19] there is no reason why one cannot replace that view with a description in which the effect attributed to the unit passive in Chafe's model is achieved without that feature. This can be accomplished by stating as optional the rules through which an actor noun root is incorporated in a configuration containing an action-process verb. The assumption is that speakers can talk of action-processes denoted by verb roots such as *kill* = *matar*, *kiss* = *beijar*, *rob* = *assaltar*, etc., as well as of experiential action-processes denoted by verb roots like *hear* = *ouvir*, *see* = *ver*, *listen* = *escutar*, etc., without necessarily having a noun root labelled actor in the semantic structures of the sentences in which those verbs appear. Thus, in sentences like those of (40), the relevant part of the appropriate semantic configurations would be something like the diagrams of (41). In both cases, the goal noun is transformed into a surface subject, and a postsemantic rule (akin to case grammar rules) states that the postsemantic processes subsumed under the label passivization (or Tpas) apply whenever a constituent other than the actor becomes the subject.

(40a) O pier foi destruído.
(40a') The pier was destroyed.
(40b) Maria foi ouvida [dizer que não viria.]
(40b') Maria was heard [to say that she would not come.]

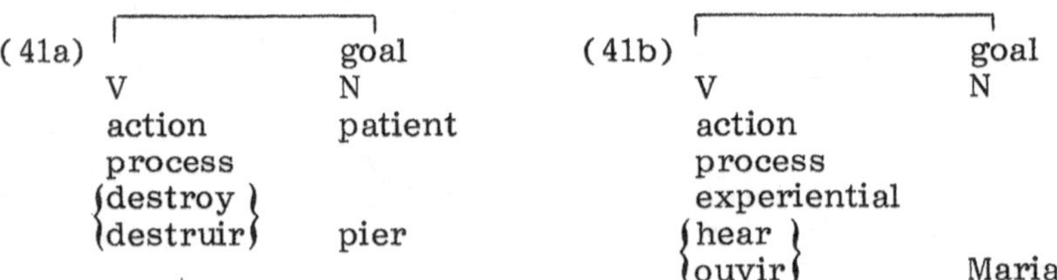

The assignment of *pier* and *Maria* as subjects in (40) has nothing to do with the presence or absence of the unit new in these roots. Passivization is obligatory in the case of semantic configurations like those of (41) because the only noun in them which can become a subject is a nonactor. In notational form, we can characterize Tpas as in (42).

(42) Tpas: V (root) ⟶ V (root, passive) /if N (-actor) ⟶ N (SJ)

It is also possible to account for the distribution of information in which the goal of a verb contains old information, while the actor contains new information, without recourse to passive as a semantic unit. This function was attributed to passive so as 'to change the order of priorities for the distribution of new information' (Chafe 1970: 220). But one must ask whether it is really necessary to have such an order of priorities at all. Its main motivation was to provide a basis for the automatic assignment of the nonnew noun to the function of subject, but even at the least marked level, the distribution of old and new information is not enough to guarantee such an automatic assignment. Consider the dialogue of (43).

(43a) I heard Mrs. Smith screaming last night. What happened to her?
(43b') Oh, she was being beaten up by her husband, as usual.
(43b") Oh, her husband was beating her up, as usual.

Both (43b') and (43b") can be related to the same semantic structure in which the actor (*husband*) and the verb (*beat up*) convey new information, while the goal (*she/her = Mrs. Smith*) contains old information. But there is no guarantee that either sentence would be chosen over the other, despite the fact that 'there is a close connection between the semantic specification of a noun root as old information...and the appearance of the noun...as a surface subject' (Chafe 1970: 240). Such connection does exist, but the speaker is free to pick out one structure or the other, although this choice may be conditioned by syntactic factors as well. In fact, it has been submitted by Weiner and Labov (1978: 19-20) that although

> given vs. new exert an effect upon the choice of active or passive in English...this result coincides with other empirical studies which indicate that such functional or semantic effects are comparatively small in relation to the syntactic factors that control the organization of the sentence.

However, these recent findings (which may or may not apply to Portuguese) do not contradict the assertion that passive sentences reflect a distribution of new vs. nonnew different from that found in nonpassive sentences.

1.4 Communicative dynamism and passivization. The third level of analysis mentioned in Table 1 has to do with the organization of information in the sentence. However, the notion of new vs. nonnew information, as used by Chafe (1970), is insufficient for our purposes, since it leaves out the fact that the elements of most utterances not only convey new or old information, but can also be classified according to their relative importance for the message.

The study of sentences from the viewpoint of distribution of information was introduced in the work of the Czech linguist Vilém Mathesius, and has been developed and refined by other linguists associated with the Prague School.[20] The basic principle at this level is that of functional sentence perspective (FSP), which controls the arrangement of sentence elements according to their degree of communicative dynamism (CD), characterized as

> the extent to which the sentence element contributes to the development of the communication, to which, as it were, it 'pushes' the communication forward (Firbas 1966a:270).

According to their degree of CD, sentence elements are organized into three general areas, namely, the theme (TH), the transition (TR), and the rheme (RH). Even though the information conveyed by the theme is frequently 'known or at least obvious in the given situation' (Mathesius, quoted in Firbas 1966a:268), its main characteristic lies in that its components, whether new or old, carry 'the lowest degree(s) of CD within the sentence' (Firbas 1966a:272). Thematic elements set up a frame of reference which serves as background for displaying new information conveyed by the rheme, that is, 'that which the speaker states about, or in regard to, the theme' (Mathesius, cited in Firbas 1966a:277). The rheme, on the other hand, represents that which is said, or predicated, about the theme. Its elements contain the highest degree of CD in the sentence, and it thus constitutes the very core of the message.

This framework allows us to classify the semantic elements of a sentence along a continuum ranging from less important to more important information. Thematic and rhematic elements, on the other hand, are bridged by transitional ones which, as regards their CD, 'rank above theme...and below rheme' (Firbas 1965:170). As to the characterization of transitional elements, it appears that in general transitive verbs often carry less CD than their complements (although more than their subjects), and thus constitute a kind of transition between thematic subjects and rhematic complements. But it is noteworthy that a verb form, once it has been analyzed in terms of semantic features, can be shown to convey both new (=rhematic) and nonnew (=thematic or transitional) information.[21] For example, in the sentence *My cat died*, considered as an answer to *Why were you crying yesterday?*, the verbal lexical unit *die* contains new information, but the verbal elements of tense and aspect convey old information, and can be traced back to their counterparts in the question.[22]

The concept of FSP presupposes the analysis of sentences in relation to their context. It just is not possible to decide about the FSP character of the elements of sentences considered in isolation, since the same surface sentence can carry different distributions of FSP, depending on its locus of occurrence in the discourse. For example, the elements of a sentence like *My daughter got married* can be analyzed in the following ways.

				(In the context defined by [= as an answer to] the question:)
(44a)	TH:	my daughter	[-new]	What about your daughter?
	RH:	got married	[new]	
(44b)	TH:	my daughter	[-new]	What did your daughter do?
		PAST	[-new]	
	RH:	get married	[new]	
(44c)	TH:	My daughter	[new]	Why are you so unhappy?
	RH:	got married	[new]	

In (44c), for instance, though both the theme and the rheme convey new information, the latter definitely has a higher degree of CD.

The basic requirement of FSP is that sentence elements be arranged in an order of increasing CD.[23] In very general terms, this means that sentence material is usually arranged in a theme-transition-rheme sequence. It happens, however, that the ultimate form of a sentence is not determined by FSP alone, but rather by the interplay of constraints which obtain at each of the three levels of sentence structure considered here. The actual organization of an utterance depends largely on language-specific rules of word order and grammatical function. For example, a language in which adjectives must precede nouns cannot depend on word order to express the difference between FSP arrangements like N^2 Adj^1 and N^1 Adj^2, where the superscript numbers indicate differences in degree of CD. Consider, for example, the English sentence *Our brave soldiers do not fear the enemy,* which can have at least two interpretations as regards the subject. If it is assumed that all of our soldiers are brave, the noun carries a higher degree of CD than the adjective, which is almost superfluous, since it denotes an implicit quality. If no such assumption is made and the sentence refers instead to 'those soldiers of ours who are brave', the adjective is essential, as it denotes that the information conveyed by the noun is limited to a subset of 'our soldiers'. Only in the first case, however, is the distribution of CD reflected directly in the linear organization of the sentence, since the English system of word order requires that adjectives precede the nouns they modify. The different meanings, however, are set apart by different intonation patterns, i.e. in either case the rhematic element will receive stronger stress: *Our brave sóldiers* vs. *Our bráve soldiers.*

Portuguese has the necessary word order rules to make sentence organization parallel the distribution of CD exemplified here. Consider the examples of (45).

(45a) [N^2 Adj^1] Nossos valentes soldados não temem o inimigo.
(45b) [N^1 Adj^2] Nossos soldados valentes não temem o inimigo.

As Firbas (1964:116f.) points out, word order is not the only means for signaling FSP, since word order depends primarily on rules spelled out at the grammatical level rather than at the level of FSP. In contrastive studies of Czech and English, Firbas (1959, 1964) demonstrates that different languages can have their FSP structure conveyed in different ways. In Czech, because of a very flexible system of rules, word order is the main principle of FSP. In English, however, word order rules often run counter to FSP requirements, which must thus be satisfied by other means, such as the use of contrasting intonation patterns.

The findings of Bolinger (1954, 1972), Daneš (1960), and Chafe (1970), among others, indicate that one of the main resources of FSP in English resides in the placement of prosodic (sentence) stress. As Bolinger (1954) shows, although there is no mechanical rule for sentence stress in English, there is a strong correlation between sentence stress placement and what he calls the 'information point' of a sentence. That information point is the rheme; in the case where there are several rhematic elements, it constitutes the rheme proper, i.e. the element of highest degree of CD. We can exemplify, following Bolinger's (1954) argument, with the following sentences.

(46) Why was the office boy so happy?
(46a) A raise was gránted.
(46b) A ráise was granted.

We can appreciate the distinction between (46a) and (46b) if we place them in the context of the following situations. In both cases, new information is being communicated about the granting of a raise (=theme). In (46a), however, the information point is the act of granting, as perhaps there was reason to wonder whether a raise would be granted at all, although there had been rumors about it. In (46b), on the other hand, emphasis is on *raise*, and we can easily imagine a situation in which raises can be expected to be automatically granted, provided that the powers-that-be make the first move to propose it. If we are willing to stretch our imagination a bit, it will not be difficult to imagine that, in the first case, someone directly interested in the raise would grasp the full content of the message simply from hearing, *It was gránted*! In the second case, just the words *A ráise*! would convey practically the whole message.[25]

A language with a more flexible system of word order, such as Portuguese, can express the differences implied in (46) in more ways than English, by means of combinations of sentence stress placement and word order. This is exemplified by the sentences of (47), in which the underline represents sentence stress.

(47a) O aumento saiu.
(47b) Saiu o aumento.
(47c) O aumento saiu.
(47d) Saiu o aumento.

A number of examples can be adduced to bear out the hypothesis that Portuguese and English differ in their utilization of prosodic stress and word order as a means of FSP. There is, for instance, the case of the rhematic subjects of the so-called 'verbs of emergence'. Whereas English must preserve the order subject-verb, Portuguese is free to use either that or verb-subject:

(48a) I was driving along the highway when a police car appeared.
(48a') Eu ia dirigindo pela estrada quando um carro de polícia apareceu.
(48a") Eu ia dirigindo pela estrada quando apareceu um carro de polícia.
(48b) I was driving along the street when the police car reappeared.
(48b') Eu ia dirigindo pela estrada quando o carro de polícia reapareceu.
(48b") Eu ia dirigindo pela estrada quando reapareceu o carro de polícia.

However, English does possess ways of making an otherwise fully new element thematic. A common device consists in the use of the (usually anaphoric) determiner *this* to thematize a new noun, thus assigning to it (or indicating that it has) a lower degree of CD than that conveyed by the remainder of the sentence:

(49) Well, I'm mad because of this salesman who came to my house a couple of hours ago.

Given the basic requirement of FSP (i.e. the sequence theme-rheme) and the largely obligatory order subject-verb-object in English, it is not surprising that the surface subject should appear as thematic in the majority of cases. Consequently, thematic actors more often than not become actualized as surface subjects.

Sometimes, however, a speaker wants to convey a message in which an actor noun is presented as rhematic. One of the ways in which this can be done consists in setting up a separate intonation contour for the subject, as in (50b), as opposed to (51b).

(50a) What happened?
(50b) ^{3}Peter^2 | ^{2}kissed ^{3}Martha^1.

(51a) What did Peter do?
(51b) ^{2}Peter kissed ^{3}Martha^1.

Another way is by making the sentence passive, and thus shifting the rhematic actor to the end of the sentence, where, in all probability, it will receive prosodic stress. However, it is not the passive construction that makes the actor rhematic, but rather the latter's degree of CD. What the passive does is to accommodate, by means of a special arrangement of surface structure elements, a distribution which parallels the theme-rheme order required by FSP.

Given a partial semantic configuration like (52), the decision as to what is thematic and what is rhematic depends on both the context and the semantic structure.[26] If the actor happens to be rhematic, on account of containing the highest degree of CD in the sentence, then the passive may be used to create a theme-rheme sequence in the surface structure, while at the same time preserving the subject-verb-object order typical of English.

(52)		goal	actor
	V	N	N
	action process	patient	agent
	kill	cop	student

The crucial question as regards theme and rheme is decided not so much by the distinction between new and nonnew elements as by their differences in CD. Clearly, new elements are rhematic. But consider the case in which, in a configuration like (52), both nouns and the verb convey new information. Such a configuration may form the basis for answers to questions of the type What's the news?, What's the matter?, What happened?, etc., which make few or no presuppositions about the content of their replies, and which therefore impose no restrictions on the distribution of theme and rheme in them. The person who provides the answers, however, must pay heed to certain facts which derive from his knowledge of the world, and which take the form of 'presuppositions about intended referents' (McCawley 1968a:267) of lexical units.

Suppose the speaker wants to give an answer including the elements *arrest*, *policeman* (actor), and *thief* (goal), all of them conveying new information. In order to do that, he has to decide what is going to be rhematic and what thematic. It happens, however, that one of the presuppositions about policemen is that they arrest people; also, a presupposition about the action of arresting is that it is carried out by law enforcement officers rather than ordinary citizens. Thus, given *policeman*, one can expect *arrest*, and vice-versa. But it is also likely, ideally at least, that the goal of an arrest is some kind of law-breaker, that is, given both *policeman* and *arrest*, one would expect *thief*, *burglar*, *assailant*, etc., rather than, say, *bishop* or *infant*. The semantic fit among the two nouns and the verb in our hypothetical answer is such that it would be difficult to say which one has a higher degree of CD. For that reason, perhaps, sentences like those of (53) are considered practically equivalent within the context of question (53a) by some native speakers of English. Similar examples can be constructed with the elements of (54).

(53a) What happened last night?
(53b) A ²policeman ²arrested a ³thief¹.
(53c) A ²thief was ²arrested by a ³policeman¹.

(54)

Verb:	Goal:	Actor:
save	swimmer	lifeguard
marry	couple	priest
put out	fire	fireman
patrol	building	watchman

A different situation is portrayed by the elements of (55), where the semantic fit is less perfect between goal and verb, in each case, than between actor and verb. Doubtless the reader will agree that policemen are less expected to arrest infants than law-breakers; that priests usually wed individuals of opposite sexes; that lawmen normally raid crime joints rather than churches. The unexpected element in (55) is always the goal, which is less predictable, given the verb and the goal, than in (54); notice, on the other hand, that, given the verb and the goal in (55), the actor is fairly predictable.

(55)

Verb:	Goal:	Actor:
arrest	infant	policeman
marry	two men	priest
raid	church	sheriff

If the elements in (55) are used to form sentences, there is a higher probability than in (54) that the less predictable goal nouns will be considered as having a higher degree of CD, and therefore they will be placed in the rheme. It is a little more natural to have the resulting sentences in the nonpassive form, as in (56). The passive is unlikely in this case; if it is used at all, the subject-goal will almost certainly be set off by a separate intonation contour, as in (57).

(56a) A ²policeman ²arrested a ³bishop¹.
(56b) A ²priest ²married two ³men¹.

(57a) A ^{3}bishop^{2} | was ^{2}arrested by a ^{3}policeman^{1}.
(57b) Two ^{3}men^{2} | were ^{2}married by a ^{3}priest^{1}.

The semantic fit of the elements of (58) is less complete between the actor and the verb than between the goal and the verb. The gist of the message lies in the fact that certain things are said to have been done by somewhat improbable actors, and therefore the actor nouns are likely to contain a higher degree of CD than the goal nouns. This situation is the reverse of that in (55): the actors being rhematic, the passive construction provides a more effective way than the nonpassive for establishing the theme-rheme order. Again, if a nonpassive is used, the rhematic subjects will probably be set off by a separate intonation contour, as in (59).

(58)	Verb:	Goal:	Actor:
	arrest	thief	elderly lady
	marry	couple	policeman
	put out	fire	infant
	beat up	bouncer	cripple
	rob	store	watchman

(59a) A ^{2}thief was ^{2}arrested by an ^{2}elderly ^{3}lady^{1}.
(59b) An elderly ^{3}lady^{2} | ^{2}arrested a ^{3}thief^{1}.
(59c) A ^{2}bouncer was ^{2}beat up by a ^{3}cripple^{1}.
(59d) A ^{3}cripple^{2} | ^{2}beat up a ^{3}bouncer^{1}.

These examples, of course, merely serve to illustrate certain apparent tendencies which, if backed by sufficient data, may be incorporated into a theory about the correlations between phenomena of 'voice' and phenomena of FSP.

1.5 Passivization and contrastive sentences. Typically, a contrastive sentence conveys the speaker's decision to set off one or more of its elements against others, which may either (a) be present in the same sentence, or (b) have been mentioned and be somehow related to what is being said, or (c) simply be implicit in the context of the conversation. Sentences (60a)-(60c) illustrate these three possibilities, with contrasts indicated in brackets.[27]

(60a) I don't want you to just *like* me, I want you to *love* me. [like:love]
(60b) I said you should *give* it to her. [give:lend]
(60c) I gave Fido the medicine you recommended and he *died*! [die:recover]

A contrastive element is often marked in English by pitch four, which besides being highest, also 'begins falling to its lowest point as soon as it has reached its highest point on the stressed syllable' (Chafe 1970:224). Contrastive pitch in

Portuguese seems to follow a similar pattern, which employs pitch level three.[28] In the sentences of (61), for example, the stressed syllable of each contrastive element is usually pronounced with high pitch, which drops to level one as soon as the stressed syllable has been pronounced, and remains at that level until the end of the intonation contour.

(61a) Elle comprou um barco. [barco:carro]
(61b) Maria foi reprovada, Lúcia é que foi aprovada. [Maria: Lúcia; aprovar:reprovar]
(61c) Eu tomei o ônibus que você me disse e ele me levou para Vila Maria! [Vila Maria:outro lugar]

According to Chafe (1970:223f.), such sentences are generated when a rule like (62) applies, optionally specifying a verb by means of the selectional unit contrastive. Furthermore, the lexical root or roots which will carry the actual contrast in the surface representation are further specified for focus, a feature which becomes actualized by means of contrastive pitch.

(62) V —— ——⊳⊳ contrastive

Another possibility, perhaps a simpler one, would consist in having the feature contrastive assigned directly to the items that carry the contrast in the surface structure, without recourse to the feature focus.

The formalization of these rules is not so important, however, as the fact that contrastive pitch corresponds, on the level of FSP, to the rhematization of whatever items are being contrasted.[29] The notion of contrastiveness applies to an element containing old information (or at any rate which is regarded as such by the speaker), which is thereby set off against another (equally nonnew) element. The novelty of a contrastive sentence resides precisely in the contrast rather than in any of the other semantic characteristics of its elements. The entire lexical unit must occupy the rhematic position (defined by the contrastive pitch contour); the truly rhematic element, nonetheless, is the feature contrastive.

In order to examine the relationships between passivization and contrastiveness, let us consider the sentences of (63) and their passive counterparts of (64), all of them contrastive. Sentences indicated by the same lower case letter are intended to be contrastive in the same way. The portions in brackets serve merely to situate the intended contrast in a plausible context.

(63a) The man killed the child [and not someone else killed the child].
(63b) The man killed the child [but not the dog].
(63c) The man killed the child [rather than caressed it].

(64a) The child was killed by the man [not by the woman].
(64b) The child was killed by the man [but the dog was not killed].
(64c) The child was killed by the man [rather than caressed].

The question is whether there is, between the sentences of (63) and their respective counterparts of (64), the same kind of difference which usually obtains between noncontrastive passives and their nonpassive counterparts. The responses of four informants indicate that no such difference exists. If that is the case, the passivized contrastive sentences of (64) do not reflect a distribution of information different from that expressed in the sentences of (63). Consequently, the semantic configurations of (63) and (64) can be represented, in an abbreviated manner, as in (65), where the distribution of the unit contrastive is indicated by the sign x.

(65)

		goal	actor
	V	N	N
		patient	agent
	kill	child	man
(63a), (64a)			x
(63b), (64b)		x	
(63c), (64c)	x		

A contrastive element can represent new information, as in the following contrastive sentence, in which the noun *policeman* receives contrastive pitch.

(66) The milk is being delivered by a policeman.

However, the fact that such a noun conveys a contrast appears to inhibit its specification as new. Perhaps as a consequence of the fact that a lexical root specified as contrastive must be actualized with high-falling pitch, regardless of its position in the sentence, whatever contrast there may be between passives and nonpassives is then masked, so to speak, by their contrastive character. Consider the sentences of (67).

(67a) Yes, I've got the milk. And guess what? Today a policeman delivered it!
(67b) Yes, I've got the milk. And guess what? Today it was delivered by a policeman!

It seems, therefore, that in a contrastive sentence the unit new does not play a decisive role in the assignment of the subject. The equivalence of contrastive passives and nonpassives is further borne out when we examine sentences containing two- and three-way contrasts, such as those of (68), whose abbreviated semantic configurations are indicated in (69).[30]

(68a) The man killed the child.
[not the wolf] [not the woman]

(68a') The child was killed by the man.
[not the woman] [not by the wolf]

(68b) The man killed the child.
[not the woman] [not caressed]

(68b') The child was killed by the man.
[not caressed] [not by the wolf]

(68c) The man killed the child.
[not caressed] [not the woman]

(68c') The child was killed by the man.
[not the woman] [not caressed]

(68d) The man killed the child.
[not the wolf] [not caressed] [not the woman]

(68d') The child was killed by the man.
[not the adult] [not caressed] [not by the woman]

(69)

	V	goal N patient	actor N agent
	kill	child	man
(68a,a')		x	x
(68b,b')	x		x
(68c,c')	x	x	
(68d,d')	x	x	x

The same equivalence between contrastive nonpassives and passives has been attested in Portuguese sentence pairs like those of (70) and (71).

(70a) O menino matou o gato.
[e não a menina]

(70a') O gato foi morto pelo menino.
[e não pela menina]

(70b) O menino matou o gato.
[e não o cachorro]

(70b') O gato foi morto pelo menino.
[e não o cachorro]

(70c) O menino matou o gato.
[e não acariciou]

(70c') O gato foi morto pelo menino.
[e não acariciado]

(71a) Eu disse que João beijou Maria.
[e não José] [e não Laura]

(71a') Eu disse que Maria foi beijada por João.
[e não Laura] [e não por José]

(71b) Eu disse que João comprou
[e não José] [e não alugou]
o apartamento.
[e não a casa]

(71b') Eu disse que o apartamento foi comprado
[e não a casa] [e não alugado]
por João.
[e não por José]

It is possible that the foregoing considerations present a somewhat simplified picture, which may have to be changed as a result of further investigation. Not all contrastive passive/nonpassive pairs examined drew the same reaction from the informants. For instance, one of them said that, in spite of the fact that the sentences of (65) seemed entirely equivalent to her, those of (72) did not strike her in the same way, although she was at a loss to tell wherein the difference lay. Other informants, however, found that the sentences of (72) were just like those of (65).

(72a) David emptied the box [and not the bucket].
(72b) The box was emptied by David [but not the bucket].

While such different reactions occurred a few times during the investigation, they were not frequent enough to totally disprove the hypothesis presented here, namely, that passivization does not have a direct bearing on the distribution of CD in contrastive sentences.

1.6 Sample derivation of a passive sentence. In order to establish some of the rules responsible for the generation of passive sentences from a given semantic configuration, let us examine the derivation of a simple Portuguese passive (73a) and its English equivalent (73b), for which very similar semantic configurations are postulated (73a')-(73b').

(73a) As pontes foram destruídas pelos soldados.

(73a')		goal	actor
	V	N	N
	action	patient	agent
	process	count	count
		feminine	potent
			animate
			human
	destruir	ponte	soldado
	new	definite	new
	past	plural	definite
			plural

(73b) The bridges were destroyed by the soldiers.

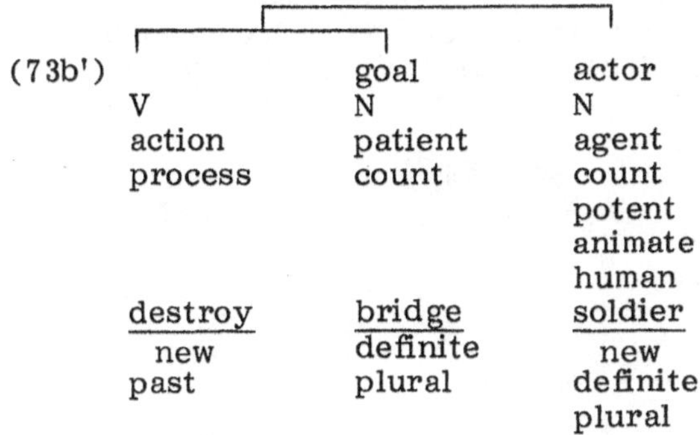

In the first place, there are the function rules (FR) which govern the assignment of surface functions. Keeping in mind what was said about the role of FSP in the selection of the subject, let us assume that the speaker has decided to make the goal noun thematic, and that therefore that noun has been chosen as subject in both (73a) and (73b). This decision determines the functions to be assigned to the remaining noun root, as shown in (FR-74). If the foregoing semantic configurations did not include actors, (FR-75) would, of course, not apply.

(FR-74) goal
N —▷ N /

(FR-75) act —▷ -act SJ
N N^{Agt} / if N — N
PrepAgt

The postsemantic configuration resulting from the application of (FR-74, FR-75) to (73a'), (73b'), and represented in the diagrams of (76a), (76b), are now ready for the literalization rules (LR) which transform certain semantic units into 'arbitrary configurations of postsemantic units before a surface structure is reached' (Chafe 1970:246).[31]

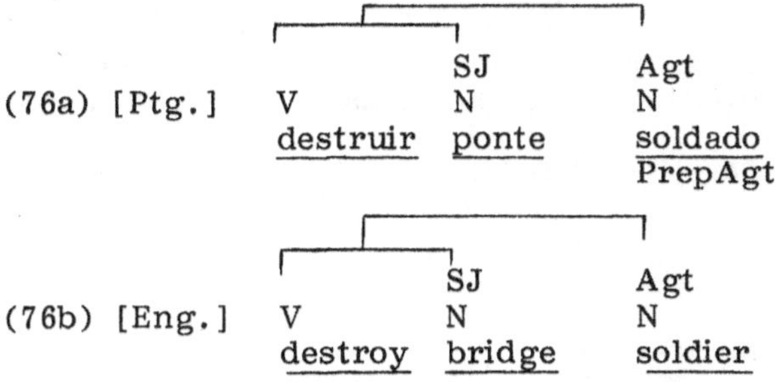

Because a noun root other than the actor has been chosen as a subject, the verb, as has been pointed out elsewhere, must be passivized. This is achieved by (LR-77), which; applied to the verb roots in (76a), (76b), yields the following partial configurations.

```
                                    -act   SJ
(LR-77)   V ─▷ V             /   N ─▷ N
          root   root
                 passive

(78a)     [Ptg.] V ──▷ V
                 destruir  destruir
                           passive

(78b)     [Eng.] V ──▷ V
                 destroy   destroy
                           passive
```

The presence of the unit passive has several consequences which are reflected in the surface structure of the verb. In the first place, it causes the original verb to become associated with a verb root which functions as an auxiliary to it, and which I call the passive auxiliary (AuxPas). Secondly, it causes units specifying the verb for tense, aspect, etc., to be transferred to the AuxPas root as postsemantic inflectional units. Furthermore, it brings about its own replacement, in the verb root, by the unit participle, whose effect is the actualization of that verb in the surface structure as a past participle. These modifications can be expressed by a rule like (LR-79).

```
                        ┌────────────┐
                                     AuxPas
(LR-79) V  ─▷  V                     V
        tense
        aspect
        root      root          root
        passive   participle    tense
                                aspect
```

On the other hand, language-specific rules such as (80a), (80b), introduce appropriate passive auxiliary verb roots.

```
                  AuxPas          AuxPas
(80a) [Ptg.]      V      ──▷      V
                                  ser

                  AuxPas          AuxPas
(80b) [Eng.]      V      ──▷      V
                                  be
```

The result of the application of rules (LR-79) and (80) to the passive verbs of (78) can be represented by the configurations of (81).

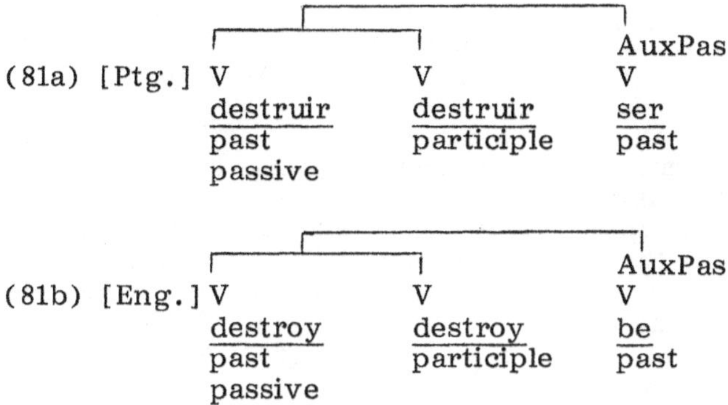

In Portuguese, the specification of the verb as a participle makes it impossible for it to serve as input to the rules of subject/verb agreement which, as is known, are obligatory. Because of that, agreement becomes a function of the AuxPas verb root which, by a rule like (LR-82) takes on the specifications of person and number present in the subject noun, and which, in a nonpassive configuration, would be copied onto the original verb.

(LR-82) [Ptg.]	AuxPas		AuxPas		SJ
	V	⟶	V	/	N
	ser		ser		
			person		person
			number		number

On the other hand, the Portuguese participle must agree in gender and number with the subject noun or pronoun, as determined by rules like those of (LR-83). The first of these states that the participle is specified as feminine if the subject consists of one or more feminine nouns; the second rule, in turn, says that the participle is inflected as plural if the subject consists of a minimum of two nonplural nouns or at least one plural noun.

(LR-83a) [Ptg.]				SJ
	V	⟶	V	/ N x
	participle		participle	feminine
			feminine	
				where x $\geq$ 1

```
                                                      SJ
(LR-83b) [Eng.]  V          ——▷  V               /  N x
                 participle      participle         (plural)
                                 plural
                                              ⎧ ≥2 if [-plural]
                                 where x      ⎨
                                              ⎩ ≥1 if [plural]
```

The subject noun in the postsemantic configuration of (76a) is specified as plural, and consequently, so is the AuxPas. However, since the subject noun is not specified for person, the AuxPas remains unmarked for that feature. This causes it to be realized in the surface structure as an (unmarked) third person form. On the other hand, the subject is specified both as feminine and plural, and the rules of (LR-83) so specify the participle. The resulting configuration can be represented as in (84).

```
                 ┌──────────────────┐
                                    AuxPas
(84) [Ptg.]      V                  V
                 destruir           ser
                 participle         past
                 feminine           plural
                 plural
```

English differs from Portuguese in that it has neither gender/number agreement rules like (LR-83) nor a person/number agreement rule like (LR-82). For the majority of English verbs, agreement can be described by a rule like (LR-85), quoted from Chafe (1970:245), which characterizes agreement as

> a surface structure suffix...symbolized s on the surface verb...and which we arbitrarily label present...and which occurs when the verb is (a) not inflected as past and (b) accompanied by a subject which is neither first person, second person, nor plural...

```
                                                   SJ
(LR-85) [Eng.]  V     ——▷▷present       /          N
                -past                              -first
                                                   -second
                                                   -plural
```

For the verb root *be*, however, a somewhat more complex rule seems to be needed. That is, if the root be is inflected as past, it is postsemantically replaced by a special lexical unit, symbolized in the surface structure by the form *was*, if it has a nonplural subject which is either specified as first person or which is neither first person nor second person; in all other cases, it is symbolized as *were*. If the root *be* is unspecified for tense, it is realized in the surface structure by the form *am* if the subject is nonplural and first person; as *is* if the subject is neither plural nor first person nor second person; and as *are* in all other cases. The foregoing can be summed up by the rules of (LR-86).

```
(LR-86a) [Eng.] V              SJ
                be  —▷ { was  / N
                past
                                 1st person

                                {[-1st person]}
                                {[-2nd person]}

                                  -plural

                         were /   elsewhere

                                  SJ
                         am   /   N
                                  1st person
                                  -plural

(LR-86b)        V  —▷  { is   /   -1st, -2nd person
                be
                -past             -plural

                         are  /   elsewhere
```

In the postsemantic configuration (76b), the subject is specified as plural and unmarked for person, and therefore the application of (LR-86) yields the configuration in (87); the resulting postsemantic configurations can be represented by the diagrams of (88).

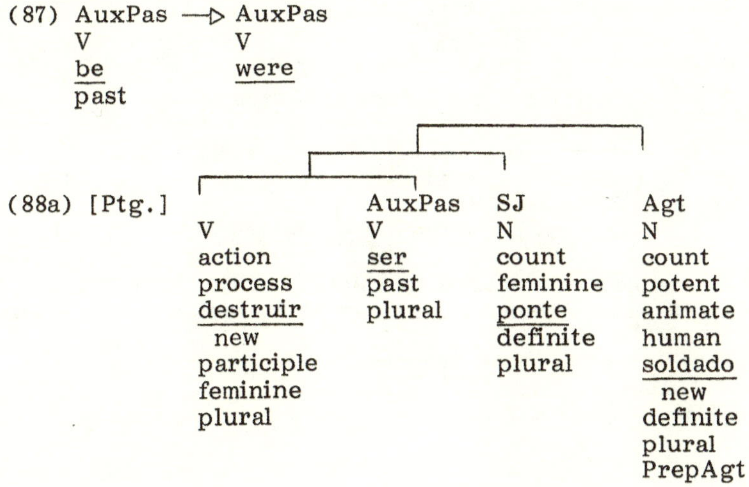

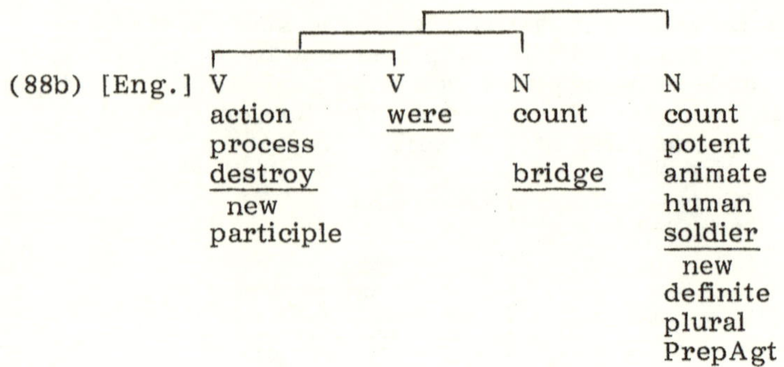

The next step involves the application of primary linearization (PL) rules, which operate on structures like those of (88), imposing on their elements an order which is reflected in the surface structure. In this chapter I am going to present only the rules which lead directly to the primary linearization of the sample sentences; further on, I look into other possible PL-rules.

Let us consider first (PL-89), which linearizes the elements which constitute the surface verb phrase. It states that an AuxPas is ordered to precede the verb root with which it is associated. Once the surface order has been determined, labels such as AuxPas, SJ, and the like are deleted automatically as no longer necessary, since word order suffices to indicate grammatical function.[32]

AuxPas
(PL-89) V_1 V_2 —▷ V_2 V_2

The application of (PL-89) to (88) would result in the partial configurations of (90).

AuxPas
(90a) [Ptg.] V destruir V ser —▷ V ser V destruir

AuxPas
(90b) [Eng.] V destroy V were —▷ V were V destroy

Next, the subject is ordered in relation to the verb phrase by a rule like (PL-91), which, applied to (88), yields (92a), (92b).

SJ
(PL-91) V_2 V_1 N —▷ N V_2 V_1

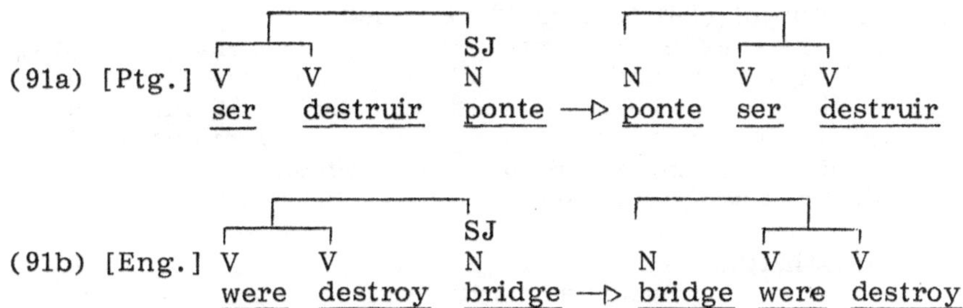

Finally, the agent noun is ordered in relation to the rest of the configuration by a rule like (PL-93), producing the configurations of (94).

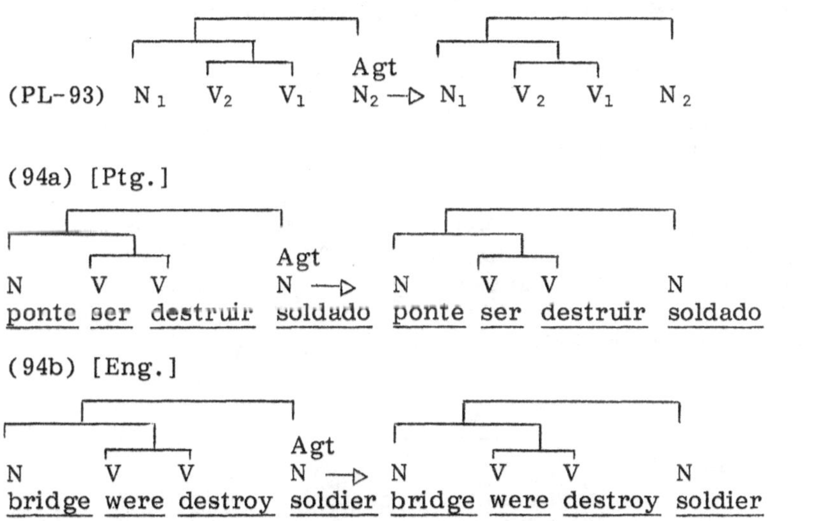

The surface order having been determined by the PR-rules, the selectional units are deleted as unnecessary by a rule like (95), in which X symbolizes any set of selectional units (Chafe 1970: 255).

(95)

$$\begin{Bmatrix} \text{N} \\ \text{V} \end{Bmatrix} \atop {\text{X} \atop \underline{\text{root}}} \longrightarrow \begin{Bmatrix} \text{N} \\ \text{V} \end{Bmatrix} \atop \underline{\text{root}}$$

In Portuguese, however, one must account for the fact that the definite article agrees with the noun in gender and number. Since gender is specified by a selectional unit, that agreement must be provided for before rule (95) deletes, as in the case of the example, the feature feminine. At this stage of the derivation, however, there is no element in the postsemantic configuration of (88) that could be called a 'definite article', for which reason the relevant agreement rule cannot yet apply. One way of accommodating this situation is by postulating a literalization rule (LR-96) which applies before all PL-rules, and which has the effect of copying the unit feminine as a postsemantic inflectional unit of a noun which is specified as feminine by a selectional unit.

(LR-96) [Ptg.] N —▷ N
feminine feminine
root root
feminine

In the case of the sample sentence, we would have the transformations shown in (97), the output of which would be substituted in the configuration of (88a), shown in (98).

SJ SJ
(97) N —▷ N
feminine feminine
ponte ponte
feminine

The application of rule (95) to the configurations of (88) would then result in the diagrams of (98), which serve as input to the secondary linearization (SL) rules which 'order the noun roots and verb roots with relation to their inflectional units' (Chafe 1970: 255).

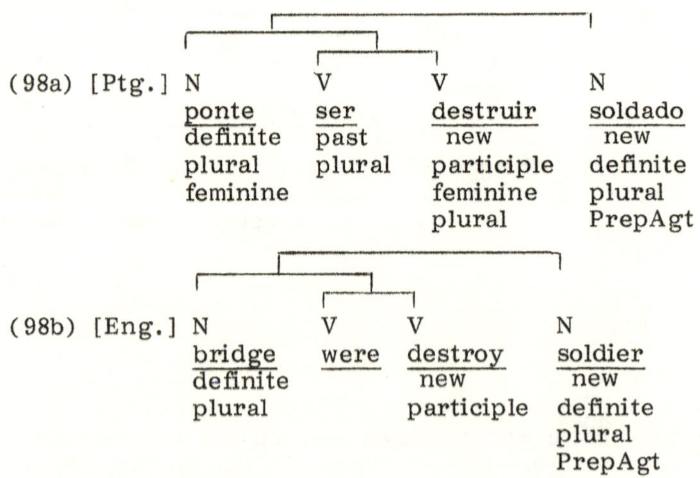

The inflectional units within a verb root are linearized by a rule like (SL-99), quoted from Chafe (1970: 256), which has the effect of placing the inflectional units, symbolized as X, after the verb root. If this rule is applied to the verbs of (98), the result will be the configurations of (100).

(SL-99) V —▷ [root X]$_V$
root
X

(100a) [Ptg.] V —▷ [[ser past] plural]$_V$
ser
past
plural

(100b) [Ptg.] V —▷ [[[destruir participle] feminine] plural]$_V$
destruir
participle
feminine
plural

(100c) [Eng.] V —▷ [destroy participle]$_V$
destroy
participle

The unit definite, on the other hand, 'is linearized to precede the noun, to become, at this stage, the item which we would identify traditionally as the definite article'; the following rule is proposed for English (Chafe 1970:246).

(SL-101) [Eng.] N —▷ [definite N]
definite

The Portuguese rule which linearizes definite has also a minor agreement function, as it copies the features feminine and plural as specifications of the unit definite.

(SL-102) [Ptg.] N —▷ [definite N]
definite (feminine) (feminine)
(feminine) (plural) (plural)
(plural)

The units feminine and plural are then linearized by the rule (SL-103).

```
(SL-103a) [Ptg.] {N        } -▷ {N        } (feminine)  (plural)
                 {definite }    {definite }
                 (feminine)
                 (plural)

(SL-103b) [Eng.] N      -▷   N          plural
                 plural
```

The linearization of the units definite, feminine, and plural would follow the steps outlined in (104).

```
                 (SL-102)              (SL-103a)
(104a) [Ptg.]   N ——▷     definite    N ——▷  def fem pl  N   fem pl
                ponte     feminine    ponte              ponte
                definite  plural      feminine
                plural                plural
                feminine

                 (SL-102)              (SL-103a)
(104b) [Ptg.]   N ——▷     definite    N ——▷  def pl    N     plural
                soldado   plural      soldado          soldado
                 new                   new              new
                definite              plural           PrepAgt
                plural                PrepAgt
                PrepAgt

                 (SL-101)              (SL-103b)
(104c) [Eng.]   N ——▷     definite    N ——▷  def      N     plural
                bridge                bridge            bridge
                definite              plural
                plural

                 (SL-101)              (SL-103b)
(104d) [Eng.]   N ——▷     definite    N ——▷  def      N     plural
                soldier               soldier           soldier
                 new                   new               new
                definite              plural            PrepAgt
                plural                PrepAgt
                PrepAgt
```

Finally, the unit PrepAgt is also linearized to precede its noun (SL-105), thereby forming an agent phrase (AG). Later on, by virtue of language-specific symbolization rules, such as (106), Prep-Agt is replaced by invariable elements identified as surface prepositions.

(SL-105) N ——▷ PrepAgt N
PrepAgt

(106a) [Ptg.] PrepAgt ——▷ por

(106b) [Eng.] PrepAgt ——▷ by

We would then have the following.

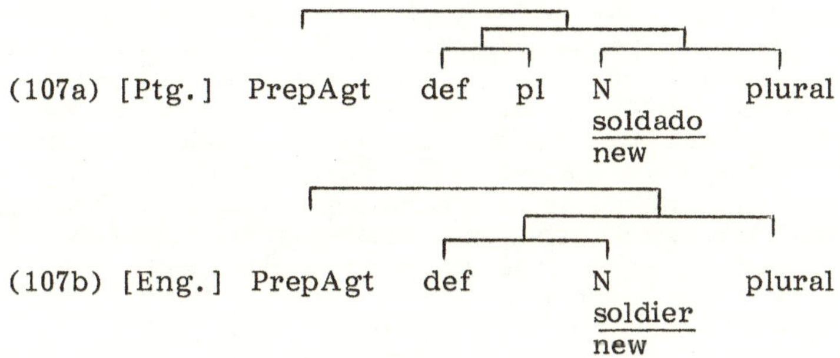

From the application of the foregoing rules, the surface structures of (108) are generated.

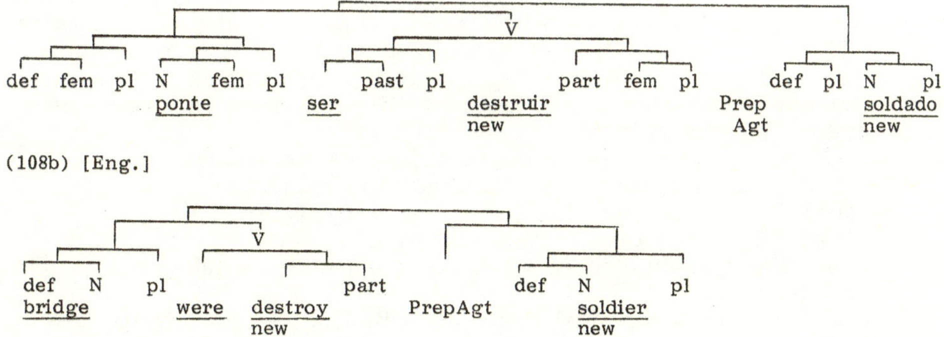

NOTES

1. Familiarity with Portuguese is presupposed on the part of the reader. Since many of the examples in this language are paralleled by examples in English, glosses will be used only when considered necessary for purposes such as disambiguation of multiple-meaning sentences, and the like. Unless otherwise

indicated, examples are my own. Those indicated by the symbol (TRC) are from tape-recorded conversations.

2. PrepAgt, which introduces the agent NP, must be specific, that is, it must be chosen from a subset of the class of English or Portuguese prepositions. The usual choices are English *by* and Portuguese *por*, other possibilities being English *of* and Portuguese *de*. The use of the latter two was more widespread in earlier stages of either language. Nowadays, *of* seems to occur with verbs of a limited semantic class, and only in learned or poetic style: 'The old preposition was *of*, which is still found, chiefly after verbs denoting mental states: beloved, scorned, admired, etc. [e.g.] Of all foresaken, and foresaking all (Dryden)' (Jespersen 1948:123). About the use of *de*, Almeida (1967:195) states that: 'Em alguns casos, em vez de *por* aparece a preposição *de*, principalmente com verbos que exprimem sentimento: "ser querido das crianças"--"ser temido dos néscios"--"ser amado de todos"--..."enjeitado da fortuna"--"Rosa tocada do cruel granizo"--"Rodeado de vários ministros"--"Desajudado da metrópole'. In some cases, the status of *de* is not clear, as in the passage: 'Uma conferência realizada em Washington...chegou a interessantes conclusões. Uma delas...prevê que em 1990 um terço da população será formado de negros e mulatos' (*Visão*, March 13, 1971, p. 17). In this case and others, it may be more accurate to interpret *formar* as a verb specified for the preposition *de*, and the apparent agent NP, *de negros e mulatos*, as a verbal complement.

Câmara (1971:218-219) indicates that *de* was common as PrepAgt in the archaic period of Portuguese, and that it was replaced by *por* in the classical period, although it is still found occasionally in the literary language. It is also possible for *de* to introduce noun phrases in sentences of the type *estar* + Vpart + Prep + NP, but even in these cases it is interchangeable with *por*. The reverse, however, does not obtain, as we can have both (ia), (ib), but not (iib), at least in those Portuguese dialects with which I am familiar.

(ia) O menino estava acompanhado pela namorada.
(ib) O menino estava acompanhada da namorada.
(iia) A casa estava vigiada por um cão pastor.
(iib) ?A casa estava vigiada de um cão pastor.

3. The question of other AuxPas elements is taken up in Chapter Two.

4. On the theoretical basis used in the present study, see principally Firbas (1959, 1961, 1964, 1965, 1966a,b), Daneš (1964, 1966), Chafe (1970), and Halliday (1970).

5. For Portuguese, see Pereira (n.d.:331). The same basic process is described in Stageberg's (1971:182) structuralist study of English grammar, with the added information that 'the subject of the active verb may be made the object of the preposition *by*, or it may be suppressed'. Palmer (1965:64), in an attempt at reaching a compromise between the 'distributionist' and the 'transformationist' approaches, offers the formula

$N_1\ V_{act}\ N_2 \longrightarrow N_2\ V_{pas}$ by N_1, and he adds that 'the point to be stressed is that the transformational relations (or, if one prefers, the relations in terms of classes of collocation) are not an additional feature that may or may not be added to the analysis. They are an integral part of it'.

6. For comment on both Lees' views on the status of *be* + *en* and on the analysis of *by* + NP as a manner adverbial, as well as for a different proposal, in TG terms, of the passive transformation, see Hasegawa (1968).

7. It did not, however, solve problems related to the insertion of *be* + *en*, or to passives formed with *get* as AuxPas. See Hasegawa (1968).

8. For Câmara, a passive 'is a sentence with a nominal subject based on an active sentence with a transitive verb' (1972: 143). Perini (1976) presents an analysis of passivization based on Chomsky (1965).

9. See Chafe (1967, 1968), and especially (1970). This chapter includes a summary of the relevant parts of Chafe (1970).

10. Chafe's notation (1970:ix) will be used in this study:

X———▷Y 'X obligatorily becomes Y'

X— —▷Y 'X optionally becomes Y'

X———▷▷Y 'X is obligatorily further specified as Y'

X— —▷▷Y 'X is optionally further specified as Y'

$\begin{pmatrix} X \\ Y \end{pmatrix}$ 'X and-or Y' (inclusive disjunction)

$\begin{Bmatrix} X \\ Y \end{Bmatrix}$ 'X or Y but not both' (exclusive disjunction)

$\begin{bmatrix} X \\ Y \end{bmatrix}$ 'if X and Y are both present'

-X 'if X is not present'

/ 'in the environment of'

11. I think it useful to distinguish between rules which introduce selectional and inflectional units, and the type of rules called configurational here. The latter describe the organization of possible semantic configurations containing noun and verb elements.

12. 'Mutation rules' in Chafe (1967).

13. The difference between the two approaches can be summarized thus. The generativist aims at establishing a system of formal rules whereby the possible sentences of a language can be formed. The nongenerativist takes whole utterances as a point of departure, and tries to identify the linguistic devices which they reflect in the context of occurrence. Daneš (1964: 36) speaks of a 'form-to-function' approach, as opposed to a 'function-to-form' one, adding that 'both procedures have their advantages and disadvantages...it is convenient to combine both methods, because they are complementary; one presupposes the other'.

14. See, for example, Bolinger (1954), Hatcher (1956a,b), and Hill (1963).

15. See Chafe (1970:Chapter 12).

16. It is often possible to decide which elements are supposed to carry new or old information by placing the sentence to be analyzed in a context such that it can be interpreted as an answer to a question. This procedure has been used in Contreras (1976), Cinque (1976), and Lo Cascio (1976), among others.

17. According to one native speaker (F. B. Agard), sentences (38b') and (38b") are necessarily equivalent. In his interpretation, the former would indicate that 'the whole thing is new as a unit, that is, there is nothing non-new', whereas in the latter 'each person is new, and so is the verb'.

18. As in the derivation proposed by Lester (1971:137, 139) for the sentences *My day was ruined* and *The accident was reported.*

19. 'There are many characteristic features of the passive voice that cannot easily be accounted for in terms of unidirectional active-passive transformations' (Svartvik 1966:166).

20. For a bird's eye view of the work of Mathesius and others, see Daneš and Vachek (1966). For a more elaborate view of the principle of functional sentence perspective (FSP), as well as for instances of its applications to linguistic analysis, see Mathesius (1928), Daneš (1964, 1966, 1967, 1968), Firbas (1959, 1961, 1964, 1966a, 1966b), Daneš and Vachek (1966), and Vachek (1966). Word order and passivization as FSP devices are mentioned in Garvin (1963:505-506).

21. The specification of transitional elements is not crucial to the present study. For a discussion of problems of transition in relation to verbal tense and modal elements, see Firbas (1965). On transition proper, see Firbas (1959).

22. Chafe's model accommodates these facts by making it possible to use the unit new to specify individual semantic units 'within a verb or a noun' (1970:212).

23. According to Firbas (1964:115), this would be due both to 'the character of human thought and...the linear character of the sentence'.

24. As for example, but not exclusively, in the case of nonthematic subjects. See Firbas (1966b).

25. We should keep in mind the probabilistic character of sentence stress placement in such cases. See Bolinger (1954, 1972).

26. The semantic structure 'operates within the section of the sentence which has remained unaffected by the context' (Firbas 1964:116).

27. In this section an underline indicates contrastive pitch.

28. This obtains in the dialects of Brazilian Portuguese with which I am familiar. According to Câmara (1972:24, note 1), phenomena of intonation in Portuguese 'have not yet been sufficiently studied in a rigorous way either in Brazil or in Portugal'.

29. See Bolinger (1952), where contrastive sentences are referred to as 'second instance sentences', and also Firbas (1959: 43, 53f.).

30. In the sentences of (68) each contrastive element is pronounced with high-falling pitch if that element is not final; 'the pitch falls part way during the pronunciation of this word, to rise again on the stressed syllable' of the next contrastive word (Chafe 1970: 226).

31. Only the elements relevant to the issue under examination are included in the diagrams.

32. The subscript numbers in (PL-89) are intended simply to indicate, after the deletion of AuxPas, which verb root is which.

2

PASSIVES AND RELATED SENTENCES

2.1 Other passive auxiliaries. The analysis presented in the preceding chapter suggests that the generation of passives in Portuguese and English can be described in terms of similar processes, insofar as their semantic structures are concerned. Whatever differences obtain are primarily the result of language-specific rules operating on postsemantic structures. Also, some of these rules are quite general and apply elsewhere in either language, independently of passivization itself. Such is the case of rules governing person and number agreement between the participle and the subject in Portuguese, or the more limited kind of agreement between the subject and the auxiliary in English.

At some point in the organization of semantic structures, the lexical item which is to function as the passive auxiliary (Aux Pas) must be chosen. Several English verbs besides *be* have traditionally been described as alternatives for this role. The more notorious ones are *get* (e.g. *He got mugged last night*), *become* (e.g. *The house became entirely destroyed*), *grow* (e.g. *He grew accustomed to her face*), *stand* (e.g. *He stood condemned*), and *rest* (e.g. *You may rest assured that we will do it*). However, alternation between *be* and these other verbs is not always free, and there are many cases in which only *be* can be used. Thus we can have, for example, *He was brought up in Seattle* and *Corn is grown in Ohio*, but not **He got brought up in Seattle* or **Corn gets grown in Ohio*.

There is not total agreement among authors who have dealt with this question, and Svartvik (1966: 93) points out that confusion in this matter is largely due to 'lack of formal criteria' for defining passives. A commonly cited criterion involves the characterization of one of those verbs as an AuxPas only when the associated participle retains its verbal value, that is, when it represents a surface verb rather than an adjective.[1] In English, sentences such as *He was married* (Jespersen 1909-1949:

4.108f.) can receive alternative interpretations, according to whether *married* is perceived as functioning as an adjective or as a verbal participle. In the former case, the sentence would be like any other of the pattern NP + copula + Adj (e.g. *He was happy*); in the latter, it would be a passive, and it could be expanded to include an agent phrase, as in *He was married by the Archbishop*.

The construction *be* + participle can thus convey two different semantic notions, that is, either a state or an action-process. Ambiguity is a consequence of the fact that for verbs like *marry* there is only one surface form which must do double duty as either a participle or an adjective. Other verbs, however, such as *dry*, have a form which denotes a state and functions as a surface adjective (1a), and another which expresses an action-process and functions as a verbal participle (1b).

(1a) The wood was dry.
(1b) The wood was dried.

In the case of semantic verbs with only one form, the possibility of adding an agent phrase to the sentence suffices to clarify the function of the verb. Also, use of *get* instead of *be* helps avoid ambiguity, since the participle in a sentence like *He got married* can only be interpreted as a surface verb. The replacement of *be* by *get*, however, is not entirely free, for *get* often carries special connotations such as speaker's attitude or inchoativeness (Lakoff 1971:154-158). Furthermore, there are also *get* + Vpart constructions which convey states, as in (2).

(2a) He got frustrated when he saw he would not finish on time.
(2b) He got accustomed to porridge while living in London.

There are some similarities between the sentences of (2) and those of (3) and (4). None can be expanded to include an agent phrase, and all of them involve certain modifications of states. In (2) and (3) one finds an inceptive process, described as an 'entry into a state' by Chafe (1970:132), who also analyzes sentences like those of (4) as containing a process verb derived from a state verb through the addition of *become*,[2] as in rule (5).

(3a) He became frustrated when he saw he would not finish on time.
(3b) He became accustomed to porridge while living in London.

(4a) The road became wide.
(4b) The room became empty.

(5) state ——▷▷ process
root ⟶ root + become

Since *frustrate* and *accustom* can be action-process verbs (e.g. *The draft frustrated my travel plans; My aunt accustomed me to getting up early*), we can use the same derivational process involved in (5) to establish a rule like (6), which forms derived state verbs from action-process verbs by adding to the latter a semantic unit which is reflected in the surface structure as either *get* or *become*.

(6) action ——▷▷ state
root ⟶ root + {get / become}

The verb *get*, then, has functions in common with both *be* and *become*; on the other hand, *be* + Vpart constructions can express either an action-process, or a state, or an entry into a state, as in (7).[3]

(7a) His plans were frustrated by the draft.
(7b) He was frustrated all of his life.
(7c) He was frustrated when he saw she would not come.

Although the construction *become* + Vpart denotes a state, many speakers of English consider it compatible with agent noun phrases, as in (8).

(8a) Bike-riding became popularized by Mayor Lindsay.
(8b) Those secret papers became publicized by one of the clerks.

It appears that such sentences constitute borderline cases between two notions, namely, an entry into a state and an action-process which brings about such an entry. It is noteworthy that the verbs in (8) are of the type which expresses an action-process derived from a state verb by means of a semantic unit represented on the surface structure by the suffix *-ize*. This unit is introduced by a rule like (9), which yields a surface verb denoting a derived action-process. This kind of formation may appear slightly anomalous, but if the relationships between *be*, *get*, and *become* are indeed as close as this analysis seems to show, syntactic blends capable of producing sentences like those of (8) should be expected to occur, although their well-formedness may not be accepted by all speakers of English.[4]

(9) state ——▷ action
root ⟶ process
root + -ize

The most common alternative to *ser* as an AuxPas is *estar*, but choice of one verb over the other goes hand in hand with important semantic differences. In the sentences of (10), for example, the gloss obscures the fundamental difference between (10a) and (10b), namely, that whereas the former describes a past action, the latter describes a past state.[5]

(10a) A catedral foi destruída.
'The cathedral was destroyed.'
(10b) A catedral estava destruída.
'The cathedral was destroyed.'

This difference has long been recognized in Portuguese grammar, although authors disagree as to whether or not sentences like (10b) should be considered passives. Elsewhere (Azevedo 1973, 1974), I have suggested that such sentences can express several types of states, depending on the semantic characterization of the main verb represented by the participle. It is important to recognize that *estar* + participle sentences fall into two broad categories. On the one hand, there are those like (10b), which describe only a state, and in which the participle functions as an adjective, just as in sentences like *A catedral estava linda* 'The cathedral was beautiful'. On the other hand, there are sentences like (11a), (11b), in which one perceives not only a state but also an underlying action or action-process which creates that state.

(11a) O quartel estava vigiado pelos terroristas.
'The barracks was watched by the terrorists.'
(11b) A cidade esteve tomada por desordeiros.
'The town was taken over by trouble-makers.'

It is important to notice that unlike sentences such as (10b), those like (11a), (11b) can take an agent phrase preceded by a preposition (PrepAgt + NP) which can only occur in sentences whose verb contains the unit action in the semantic structure. The paradox apparent in the cooccurrence of the notions of action and state in the same verb can be explained by derivational units[6] such as deactivative and deprocessive (Chafe 1970: 131-133), whose function consists in removing the units action and process from the original semantic specification of a verb, thus creating a derived state verb, as in (12).

(12) process —— —— state [derived]
action
<u>root</u> <u>root + deactivative + deprocessive</u>

Different types of derived states are exemplified by the sentences of (13) and (14).

(13) A casa estava acabada.
'The house was finished.'

(14a) O quartel estava tomado pelos revoltosos.
'The barracks was taken by the rebels.'
(14b) Tais atos estavam condenados pela nossa sociedade.
'Such acts were condemned by our society.'

The basic difference here is that the state expressed in (13) has a quality of permanence about it, such that once the state comes into existence, it goes on existing of its own accord. On the contrary, states like those expressed by (14a), (14b) exist only as long as they are maintained by a coexisting action (as in 14a) or by the persisting effects of an earlier action (14b); when either the action or its effects ceases to operate, the state also ceases to exist, and the element represented by the subject noun reverts to its original state. This difference accounts for the possibility of having sentences like (15), but not (16).

(15a) O quartel não estava mais tomado pelos revoltosos.
'The barracks was no longer taken by the rebels.'
(15b) Tais atos já não estavam condenados pela nossa sociedade.
'Such acts were no longer condemned by our society.'
(16) *A casa não estava mais acabada.
'The house was no longer finished.'

My original analysis (Azevedo 1974) of derived states included the units autonomous vs. dependent, with dependent states classified as either reversible or irreversible. However, it appears that the unit irreversible is sufficient. Whether or not a given verb can be so marked depends on its semantic characterization, which may vary slightly according to context, as well as according to individual speakers' perception of the nature of the state involved. An action which brings an entirely new object into existence creates more than just a state, and in such cases the use of *estar* + participle is not unanimously accepted by native speakers, as in the sentences of (17).

(17a) ?Esta casa está construída por um arquiteto famoso.
'This house is [i.e. 'has been'] built by a famous architect.'
(17b) ?Este quadro está pintado por Picasso.
'This painting is [i.e. 'has been'] painted by Picasso.'

If the verb is in the past, as in (18), rejection is practically unanimous, and speakers indicate they would rather use *ser* + participle instead.

(18a) *A casa estava construída por um arquiteto famoso.
'The house was [i.e. 'had been'] built by a famous architect.'

(18b) *O quadro estava pintado por Picasso.
'The painting was [i.e. 'had been'] painted by Picasso.'

That the states expressed by the sentences of (17) are irreversible is sufficiently underscored by the impossibility of transforming these into the pattern represented by the sentences of (15), as shown in (19).

(19a) *A casa não estava mais construída por um arquiteto famoso.
'The house was no longer built by a famous architect.'
(19b) *Esse quadro não está mais pintado por Picasso.
'This painting is no longer painted by Picasso.'

If the action expressed by the verb adds a new semantic feature to an existing object, the resulting state of the latter may be seen as reversible, and thus we can have, for example, the following.

(20a) [action] A cerca foi pintada pelo João.
'The fence was painted by João.'
(20b) [resulting state] A cerca está pintada pelo João.
'The fence is [i.e. has been] painted by João.'

If the paint peels off or is washed off by a sudden storm, pattern (15) becomes a possibility, as shown in (21), although in such cases the use of PrepAgt + NP tends to be rejected by native speakers, as in (22).

(21) A cerca não está mais pintada.
'The fence is no longer painted.'
(22) *A cerca não está mais pintada pelo João.
'The fence is no longer painted by John.'

There seems to be a gradation between sentences with *ser* + participle, on the one hand, and sentences with *estar* + participle, on the other, depending on whether the dominant unit is action or (derived) state, and on whether the occurrence of PrepAgt + NP is possible or not. However, both sentence types can be ascribed to the same generative process, and neither *ser* nor *estar* need be included in the semantic representation; rather, they are introduced postsemantically, and the choice between them depends essentially on the presence or absence, respectively, of the unit state in the semantic representation of the main verb.

In order to account for the similarities between sentences of these two types, we can offer a structural definition of passives, summarized in (23).

(23) NP:SJ + Aux + Vpart + (PrepAgt + NP:Agt).

In this formula, NP:SJ is formed by an element other than the actor in the semantic structure; Vpart is either an action-process verb or a derived state verb created from an action-process verb to which the units deactivative and deprocessive have been added; Aux is either a verb form introduced post-semantically (*be, ser, estar*) which serves as a carrier of features otherwise borne by the verb in a nonpassive sentence (tense, aspect, person, number), or a verb introduced in the semantic structure as a derivational unit added to the verb root (*get, become*); PrepAgt is a language-specific preposition which introduces NP:Agt, which is a surface agent corresponding to the actor noun(s) in the semantic structure.

By having passives generated independently, this analysis avoids the thorny question of whether passives are derived from actives. What triggers passivization as a series of post-semantic operations is the choice of an element other than the actor as the surface subject. This choice is obligatory if there is no semantic actor or if there is in the semantic structure a derived state verb incompatible with such an actor.

2.2 Actor indeterminacy. I have distinguished between two types of agentless passives, namely, those deriving from an actorless semantic configuration and those which arise from deletion of the agent phrase. The question of which of these types a sentence like *Maria foi vista na praia* 'Maria was seen on the beach' belongs to can only be answered if the sentence is part of an ampler context. Consider, for example, the dialogues of (24) and (25).

(24a) A faxineira já acabou o serviço. Ela pode ir embora?
'The cleaning woman is through with the work. Can she go home?'
(24b) Não pode, ainda não.
'No, not yet.'
(24c) Mas por que? A limpeza já foi toda feita!
'But why not? All of the cleaning has been done!'

(25a) Acho que não podemos atravessar o rio hoje.
'I think we can't cross the river today.'
(25b) Por que não?
'Why not?'
(25c) A ponte foi destruída durante a noite.
'The bridge was destroyed during the night.'
(25d) Como foi isso?
'How did that happen?'
(25e) Sei lá. Só sei que foi destruída.
'Search me. All I know is that it was destroyed.'

In (24c) the verb can be interpreted as having--in the speaker's mind at any rate--a well-defined actor, namely, the *faxineira* mentioned in (24a). Although there is no way of proving that (24c) necessarily derives from something like *A limpeza já foi feita toda pela faxineira*, the context leaves no doubt that, were an agent phrase to be inserted in (24c), this would be *pela faxineira*. In (25c), (25e), however, there is no reason to suppose that either sentence has undergone a process of agent-deletion, nor that there is an actor lurking somewhere in the semantic configuration. All the speaker wants to convey--in fact, all that he can convey, given what he knows--is the notion of the destruction of the bridge during the preceding night. Clearly, there must have been an agentive cause of the destruction, since the action-process denoted by *destruir* cannot occur without one. In order to express such an occurrence, however, it is not necessary to generate a semantic structure with an actor which is deleted afterwards. An action-process can be incorporated into the grammar without being obligatorily associated with an actor noun; if this happens, passivization takes place obligatorily before the surface structure is reached, as a consequence of a constituent other than the actor having become the subject.

Besides this case of actor indeterminacy in which there is no actor noun in the semantic structure, there are also sentence types in which the actor is indeterminate by virtue of being incompletely specified in the semantic structure. This is the case with the sentences of (26).[7]

(26a) Mas será que a gente chega a tempo?
'But will we get there on time?' (TRC)

(26b) É a tal história: a televisão abusa da liberdade e depois o pessoal reclama da censura.
'It's the old story: television abuses its freedom and then people complain about censorship.' (TRC)

(26c) A turma sempre joga nesse terreno baldio.
'People usually play soccer in that empty lot.' (TRC)

(26d) Quando uma coisa é repetida demais, você acaba não acreditando naquilo, não é?
'When something is repeated too often, you end up not believing it, isn't that so?' (TRC)

(26e) Se o cara não quer barulho, tem que calar a boca.
'If a guy does not want trouble he has to shut up.'

(26f) Eu fui à Feira da Espanha há duas semanas no Anhembi. Estavam servindo uns calamares com pimenta.
'I went to the Spanish Fair at Anhembi two weeks ago. They were serving some peppered squids.' (TRC)

(26g) Lá não se brincava, se estudava!
'There one did not play around, one studied!' (TRC)

(26h) Vende-se um apartamento mobiliado.
'A furnished apartment for sale.'

(26i) O Nelson é o único de nós que ainda não foi mordido.
'Nelson is the only one of us who has not been bitten yet.'
(26j) A grama já foi comida.
'The grass has already been bitten.'
(26k) Aqueles mamões ainda não foram comidos.
'Those papayas have not been eaten yet.'
(26l) As árvores foram derrubadas.
'The trees have been felled.'

These sentences share a certain element of vagueness as to the characterization of the actor. We perceive in them a continuum of uncertainty, different shades of vagueness which grow denser as we go down the list, until the information on the actor becomes virtually nil. They also share other characteristics as well, since in all of them the actor is potent and animate (since they all involve action verbs) and in (26a)-(26h) the actor is also human, as the verbs refer to typically human actions.

As the gloss indicates, (26a) should be interpreted to mean that its speaker is included in the actor. This has been noticed by some authors, e.g. Vázquez (1961: 475).

> Conservando un ligero matiz impersonal, *a gente* 'la gente' se emplea en lugar del pronombre de primera persona del plural *nós* 'nosotros' con el verbo en tercera persona del singular (aunque popularmente pueda oírse también con el verbo en la primera del plural: *A gente não somos tolos*).

Sentences (26b), (26c) are ambiguous, as they may be interpreted as referring to a specific group of people technically called *o pessoal* 'the personnel' and *a turma* 'the gang', as in *o pessoal do escritorio* 'the office personnel' and *a turma de trabalho* 'the work crew'. In the interpretation which interests us here, however, those expressions do not denote more than a collective actor among whose number the speaker is not explicitly included.

Sentence (26d) is likewise ambiguous, but leaving aside the interpretation of *você* as a second person singular referent, we find that this word conveys a general meaning of 'indeterminate actor' paralleled in English by unstressed you /yə/.[8] The same can be said of *o cara* in (26e). In neither sentence is the hearer or the speaker included in the range of the indeterminate actor. Sentence (26f) also has an actor that is neither the speaker nor the hearer, but rather someone else--that is, it is unmarked for person and thus realized as a third person verb form. Also, there is no reason to assume that a plural actor is implied; however, use of the singular *ele* 'he', deleted or not, would necessarily imply a specific referent, and the sentence would no longer be an instance of actor indeterminacy. In the plural, *eles* 'they' may be deleted regardless of whether it is an actor indeterminacy marker or a pronoun with anaphoric value.

Sentences (26g), (26h) are even vaguer, and all they tell us is that someone (grammatical person and number unspecified) used to study rather than play around (26g) or has an apartment for sale (26h). The next two are agentless passives of the type already studied. When we compare them to the other sentences of (26), we realize that they represent an extreme case of subject indeterminacy, as nothing is known about the actor, in (26j), (26k), except that it is animate. Since *comer grama* 'to eat grass' is not an action normally performed by humans, there is a good probability that, unless the speaker is, say, King Nebuchadnezzar's gardener, he must have a nonhuman actor in mind. In (26k), however, the speaker may be referring to the damage done to the papayas in his garden by either birds or street urchins, and thus he might have in mind either a nonhuman or a human actor. Again, unless these sentences are inserted into a larger context, nothing warrants positing an underlying actor noun in either of them.

Except for agentless passives, the other types of sentences can be explained in terms of variations of the same basic configuration (27), modified to express varying cases of actor indeterminacy.

(27) N
potent
animate
human
indeterminate

2.2.1 A gente, a turma, o pessoal. While the first of these expressions can be optionally specified to include the hearer (P-2), the other two cannot. Thus, while (28a) can be paraphrased as (28b), sentences (29a), (29b) can only be paraphrased as (29c).

(28a) A gente queria permissão para usar a sala.
(28b) Nós queríamos permissão para usar a sala.

(29a) O pessoal queria permissão para usar a sala.
(29b) A turma queria permissão para usar a sala.
(29c) Eles queriam permissão para usar a sala.

The specification of these agents is expressed by rule (30).

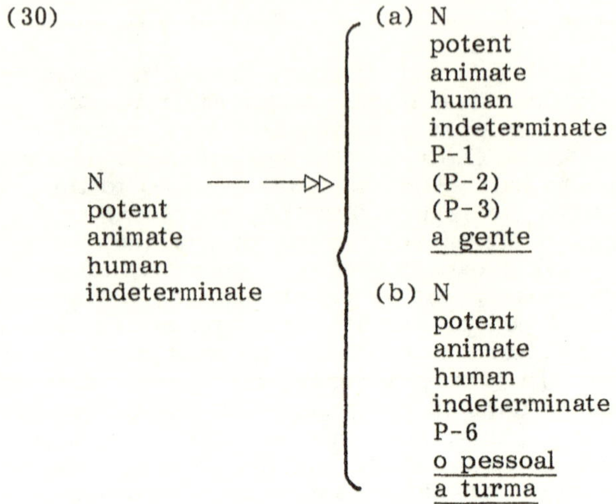

2.2.2 **Você.** A possible rule for the semantic specification of nonspecific *você*, which excludes P-1 without necessarily including P-2, would be as in (31).

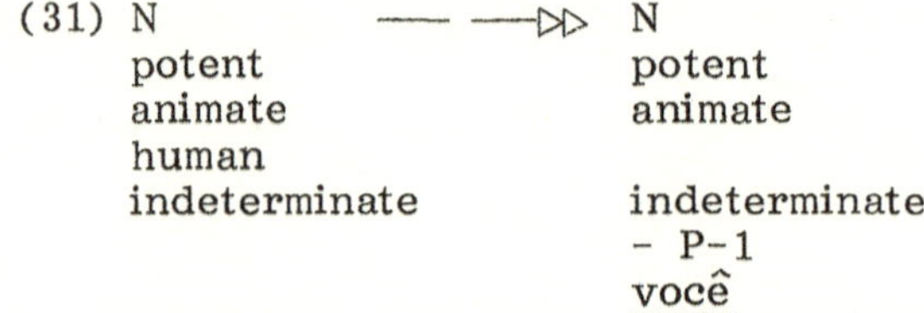

2.2.3 **O cara.** This actor indeterminacy marker excludes both the speaker and the hearer and refers to the third person without further specification. It may be pluralized, usually as *os cara* rather than *os caras* , which is not surprising, considering that this expression is typical of colloquial speech.[9] The relevant semantic configuration would be (32).

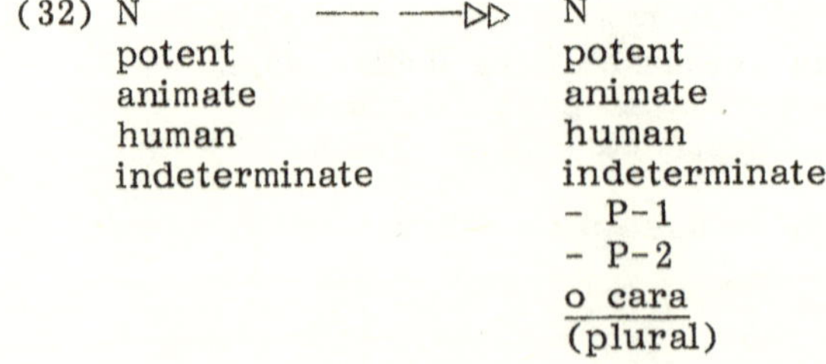

2.2.4 **Eles.** The third person plural pronoun *eles* differs from the pronouns of first and second persons in that it is diachronically a demonstrative (<Lat. *ille*) and synchronically an anaphoric which refers to a plural noun already mentioned

or at least implicit in the context. Thus, *eles* carries a full semantic content only when it is relatable to somebody or something specified, as in (33a), but not as in (33b).

(33a) Os oficiais chegaram e eles [= os oficiais] dizem que vão ficar.
'The officers have arrived and they [= the officers] say they are going to stay.'

(33b) Eles [≠ os oficiais] estão dizendo que os oficiais estão naquele hotel.
'They [≠ the officers] are saying the officers are in that hotel.'

The relevant rule would be (34).

(34)	N	——— ——⊳⊳	N
	potent		potent
	animate		animate
	human		human
	indeterminate		indeterminate
			- P-1
			- P-2
			eles
			(plural)

2.2.5 The indeterminate se. There is a wide variety of scholarly opinion on the functions of the indeterminate pronoun *se*. Some authors label sentences like those of (35) and (41) as personal passives, and those of (42) as impersonal passives (Pereira n.d.: 320-321, Bueno 1944: 382-383).[1] Others make a distinction between the use of *se* as a passivizing particle or pronoun, as in (42), or as a subject indeterminacy marker, as in (35) (Almeida 1967: 204-205, Brandão 1963: 315-319). Still others reject the notion of the passivizing function of *se* and characterize this pronoun as a marker of indeterminacy exclusively (Lacerda 1966: 77-78 and particularly Ali 1966: 89-91, to whose insights this analysis owes a great deal).

The use of *se* to make the subject indeterminate, according to Dias (1959: 106), was once commoner in sentences with transitive verbs (as well as with transitive verbs used intransitively), and it was later extended to state verbs, in 'português moderníssimo, por falsa analogia com o francês *on est heureux*', as in (35).

(35a) Vive-se bem aqui.
'One lives well here.'

(35b) Muito se sofre qhando se é honesto.
'One suffers a lot when one is honest.'

(35c) Está-se otimamente neste recanto tranquilo.
'One is very well in this quiet spot.'

(35d) Previne-se aos presentes que é proibido fumar.
'One warns those present here that smoking is forbidden.'

Although the indeterminate *se* is a well-established feature of Portuguese, some of its uses have occasionally met with the disapproval of grammarians, as the following quotation from Almeida (1967:207-208) indicates.

> Erro pernicioso e cada vez mais encontradiço em nossa literatura é o emprego da partícula *se* sem função [sic] ou, o que não é menos mau, com função errada. Diàriamente, quando não várias vêzes por dia, num mesmo jornal, num mesmo artigo, lemos construções... em que o *se* está de mais, ora por lhe não caber função, ora por desempenhar papel errado ou desnecessario:[10]

(36a) É preciso pensar-se nisso.
'It is necessary for one to think about this.'

(36b) O saber-se se o empregado quis a despedida...
'One's knowing whether the employee wanted to be laid off...'

(36c) O sonhar-se de dia...
'One's day-dreaming...'

(36d) Não é preciso cogitar-se desse caso.
'One need not consider this case.'

(36e) Era de ver-se a algazarra.
'One should see the racket.'

(36f) Analisar lògicamente uma palavra é considerar-se a palavra quanto à função...
'To analyze a word logically means for one to consider the word as to its function...'

(36g) No momento de estourar-se a bomba...
'At the moment when the bomb was going to explode ...'

(36h) No juntar-se as folhas, notou o escrivão a falta de uma.
'As the sheets were gathered, the notary noticed that one of them was missing.'

(36i) Não é possível duvidar-se da autenticidade da carta.
'One cannot doubt the authenticity of the letter.'

(36j) Era uma delícia ver-se o menino falar.
'It was delightful for one to see the boy talk.'

However, 12 informants, all of them college-educated native speakers of Brazilian Portuguese, have agreed that the sentences of (36) are acceptable and well formed. It appears that Almeida's position is strictly prescriptive and does not accurately reflect the facts of the language.[11]

The answer to the question of whether or not *se* should be considered the subject of sentences like those of (36) depends on how we define the notion of subject. If we think in terms of surface representation alone, then it may be difficult to maintain that *se* is the subject. It is feasible, nonetheless, to characterize the indeterminate *se* as the surface realization of a type of incompletely specified semantic actor.

Besides the unit indeterminate, the semantic characterization of *se* requires the unit human, since *se* cannot be associated with verbs expressing nonhuman actions, as shown by the examples of (37).

(37a) Canta-se muito na vizinhança.
'One sings a lot in the neighborhood.'
(37b) Dorme-se nem neste hotel.
'One sleeps well in this hotel.'
(37c) *Crocita-se muito neste bosque.
'*One caws a lot in these woods.'
(37d) *Come-se muito feno nesta fazenda.
'One eats a lot of hay on this farm.'

The indeterminate *se* also lacks specifications such as feminine, count, and so on, and additional features may be necessary to explain its syntactic behavior.[12] Although it is homonymous with the reflexive pronoun *se*, and despite a diachronic relationship between them, the two *se*'s are quite different from each other semantically. In fact, a case might be made to describe the indeterminate *se* as a root that has undergone an idiomatization process (Chafe 1970, Chapter 9). The relevant semantic configuration may be diagrammed as in (38).

(38) N ⟶▷▷ N
agent
animate
human
indeterminate

And, postsemantically, it is given as in (39).

(39)	N	⟶▷	N
	agent		agent
	animate		animate
	human		human
	indeterminate		indeterminate
			se

The semantic configuration of a sentence like *Trabalha-se aqui* would be represented as in (40).

		actor
(40)	V	N
	action	agent
		human
		indeterminate
	trabalhar	se

The same analysis can be extended to sentences like those of (41), which include potentially transitive action-process verbs used intransitively.

(41a) Come-se muito aqui.
(41b) Naqueles tempos, caçava-se à vontade.

There is no reason why the introduction of a goal in the sentences of (41)--which yields those of (42) and their partial semantic configurations of (43)--should interfere with the characterization of *se*.

(42a) Come-se muito peixe aqui.
(42b) Naqueles tempos, caçava-se índio à vontade.

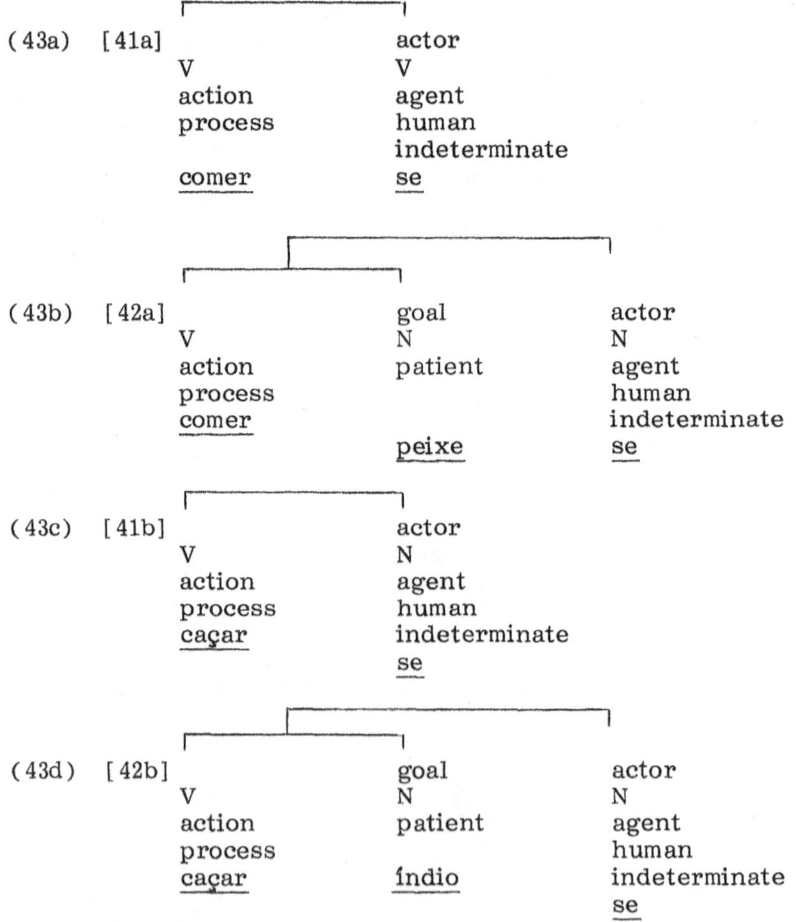

However, the use of *se* in sentences like those of (42) has received a different interpretation from some authors, who have characterized it as a 'passivizing element'. Those sentences would then be variants of the passives of (44).

(44a) Muito peixe é comido aqui.
(44b) Naquele tempo, índio era caçado à vontade.

As regards this, Brandão (1963:313) states:

> Como pronome apassivante usa-se o *se* unido a verbos transitivos para denotar que a ação por êstes significada não é exercida pelos seres aos quais êles se referem, ou por incapazes de praticá-la, ou por se manifestamente passivo o sentido [e.g.] 'Sabei que uma vasta conjuração se trama contra vós'.

On the same line of thought, and perhaps a little more explicitly, Vázquez (1961:484) says that

> ...la concordancia normal del verbo con el sujeto pasivo, en las oraciones que lo poseen, muestra bien claro que se trata simplemente de una partícula apasivante en ocasiones impersonalizadora...

According to the 'passive *se*' theory, there would be total semantic equivalence between the two types of sentences exemplified in (42) and (44), and consequently, they would all be passives. Furthermore, the subject of the sentences of (42) would be the semantic goal of the verb (*muito peixe* and *índio*, respectively), and *se* would be simply a device for passivizing the sentences.

However, passives and indeterminate *se* sentences are not always interchangeable. For one thing, there is the requirement that even the so-called passive *se* be associated only with human actions, as shown in (45).

(45a) Toda a salada já foi comida.
'All the salad has already been eaten.'
(45b) Já se comeu toda a salada.
'All the salad has already been eaten' or
'One has already eaten all the salad.'
(45c) Todo o feno já foi comido.
'All the hay has already been eaten.'
(45d) *Já se comeu todo o feno.
*'One has already eaten all the hay.'

There is also the fact that modern Portuguese does not allow the cooccurrence of *se* constructions and *por* + NP agent phrases, although this was possible in earlier periods of the language (Naro 1976:780-781). The incomplete semantic equivalence of the two sentence types suggest that they should be considered surface manifestations of different semantic structures. Even if one were to disregard the crucial distinction between human and nonhuman, there would still be enough evidence that passives are not always equivalent to their analogs with the indeterminate *se*, as is shown by the examples of (46), quoted by Naro (1976:601) from Silveira (1943).

(46a) A mesma mulher não é amada duas vezes.
'The same woman is not loved twice.'
(46b) Não se ama a mesma mulher duas vezes.
'One does not love the same woman twice.'

As Naro points out, (46a) has two readings, namely, '(a) a given person does not love the same woman on two separate occasions; or (b) once a given person has loved a woman, nobody...will love the same woman on a second occasion'. However, in (46b), 'only the first meaning is present'.

Examples (47) and (48) reinforce the view of the nonequivalence of the two sentence types.

(47a) Não se destroem essas florestas sem sofrer as consequências desse ato.
'One does not destroy these forests without suffering the consequences of this act.'
(47b) *Essas florestas não são destruídas sem sofrer as consequências desse ato.

(48a) Não se pode amar uma mulher sem desejá-la.
'One cannot love a woman without desiring her.'
(48b) *Uma mulher não pode ser amada sem desejá-la.
'A woman cannot be loved without desiring her.'

Consider now the examples of (49).

(49a) Essas florestas não são destruídas sem que as consequências desse ato sejam sofridas.
'These forests are not destroyed without the consequences of such an act being suffered.'
(49b) Uma mulher não pode ser amada sem ser desejada.
'A woman cannot be loved without being desired.'

The meanings of (49a) and (49b) differ from the meanings of their analogs with *se*, respectively (47a) and (48a). The difference consists in that, while in (47a) and (48a) the actor of the main clause is the same as the actor in the subordinate clause, in (49a) and (49b) this is not necessarily the case. It is possible to interpret (49a) as meaning that the consequences of the destruction of forests are to be suffered by someone other than the person or persons responsible for the destruction.

Likewise, (49b) can mean that a woman cannot be loved by someone unless she is also desired by someone else. The reason for these interpretations lies precisely in the fact that the sentences of (49) are agentless passives with no semantic actor, and consequently there is no requirement that either be interpreted in such a way that both the main and the subordinate clauses imply one and the same actor.

The possibility of agreement between the verb and the surface manifestation of a plural semantic goal, exemplified in (50a), (50b) has traditionally been interpreted as sufficient evidence to ascribe to this goal the role of grammatical subject. The same line of reasoning has led grammarians to reject sentences like (50c), (50d) as ungrammatical. Prescriptive rules notwithstanding, it is a fact that the agreement rules required to form (50a), (50b) are not always applied by native speakers, and sentences like (50c), (50d) are so common that only extreme normativism can justify labelling them as ungrammatical. Lack of agreement is particularly common when the semantic goal consists of more than one noun, as in (50e), (50f).

(50a) Louvaram-se os presidentes.
'The presidents were praised.'
(50b) Mataram-se os escravos.
'The slaves were killed.'
(50c) Louvou-se os presidentes.
'The presidents were praised.'
(50d) Matou-se os escravos.
'The slaves were killed.'
(50e) Destruiu-se o jardim e a igreja.
'One destroyed the garden and the church.'
(50f) Fala-se o catalão e o francês no Roussillon.
'Catalan and French are spoken in the Roussillon.'

The sentences of (50)-(52) illustrate agreement variation. The actor which would normally become the surface subject is indeterminate and represented by *se*, which, being unspecified for number, cannot serve as a basis for determining verbal agreement. Consequently, the semantic goal has been traditionally interpreted as the subject. Naro (1976:788, note 22) shows that the agreeing *se* construction, that is, the so-called '*se* passive, with agreement and agent phrase, precedes the *se*-impersonal...by several centuries', and that the nonagreeing construction was an innovation which 'gained general acceptance sometime between the mid-15th century and the mid-16th century' (Naro 1976:798); furthermore, 'the new construction has no formal connection whatever with either of the transformations that were critically involved in the derivation of its diachronic ancestor, the *se*-passive' (Naro 1976:801). Rather, the rise of the impersonal *se* constructions without agreement was linked with a new interpretation of *se* as the subject of the verb (that is, as the semantic actor) of an active construction.

This new interpretation was probably reinforced by the ambiguity involved in sentences in which the pronoun *se* can be interpreted alternatively as a marker of actor indeterminacy or as a reflexive clitic. Thus, sentences (50a), (50b) can also receive the glosses [50a] 'The presidents praised themselves/ each other', and [50b] 'The slaves killed themselves/each other'. Lapa (1970:146) remarks that, because of this possibility of multiple interpretations,

> ...dava-se uma confusão, que a língua tratou de evitar muito simplesmente: em vez de pôr o verbo no plural, como mandam as regras, empregou-o no singular, como impessoal...o pronome reflexo [i.e. *se*] foi considerado equivalente a um pronome indefinido: 'alguém', 'uma pessoa'. O processo é engenhoso e nada repugna à índole da língua...simplesmente, a construção, usada nas esferas populares, não está abonada pelos gramáticos...

The controversy on the relationship between passives and sentences with the indeterminate *se* stems from confusion between surface syntactic structures and semantic content. Those authors who consider sentences of the latter kind as a variety of the former rely mainly on the fact that there is often some semantic overlap between sentences of the two types. In doing so, they implicitly characterize passivization as a semantic, rather than postsemantic, phenomenon. Furthermore, this position requires a definition of passives as sentences in which the subject 'undergoes' rather than performs the action denoted by the verb. However, the definition of subject belongs properly to the description of surface syntactic structures, rather than to the characterization of semantic functions. If both (51a) and (51b) are passives, (or, alternatively, the same passive under two different surface representations) with the same subject (*casas*), then some formal basis must be provided for establishing the relationship between the two representations and accounting for the presence of *se* in (51a).

(51a) Venderam-se as casas.
(51b) As casas foram vendidas.

Assuming that this can be done satisfactorily, we would have to interpret (52) as a deviant construction, but this goes against the facts of the language.

(52) Lá não só se estudava os autores como também se lia os livros. (TRC)
'There one not only studied the authors but also read the books.'

Also, the pronoun *se* would have to receive different interpretations in (41) and (42), which would not be a satisfactory solution, since the difference between those sentences, as perceived by native speakers, lies in the presence of a goal in the latter, but not in the former. There is also the fact that the indeterminate *se* can cooccur with the passive construction (that is, with both *ser* + Vpart and *estar* + Vpart) in the same sentence, as in (53) and (54), which cannot be explained in terms of the traditional *se* passive.

(53a) É-se tentado pelo diabo [Naro 1976:784].[13]
'One is tempted by the devil.'
(53b) No meu tempo de jovem, era-se convidado às melhores casas de família. (TRC)
'In my youth one was invited to the best family homes.'
(53c) Era-se chamado à atenção pelas mínimas faltas.
'One was reprimanded for the slightest faults.'

(54a) Quando se está premiado pela loteria, recebe-se o prêmio.
'When one is awarded a prize by the lottery, one collects the prize.'
(54b) Se se estava sorteado, servia-se, e pronto.
'If one was drafted into the army one served, and that was that.' (TRC)

In the position put forth here, sentences with the actor indeterminacy marker *se* arise from semantic configurations which contain an incompletely specified actor noun, represented in the surface structure by that pronoun. If a plural goal noun is present, it becomes the direct object, although its interpretation as subject (of what is, essentially, a subjectless sentence) may lead optionally to making the verb agree with it. The semantic overlap and partial *se* functional interchangeability between agentless passives and indeterminate *se* sentences does not imply total identity, and rather than resort to an explanation of the type 'x is actually y', we should simply accept that certain basically different sentence types can often contain enough semantic similarity to be functionally synonymous in actual usage.[14]

Despite the differences between them seen so far, indeterminate *se* sentences and passives are sometimes so close in meaning that one would be hard put to interpret the choice between them. It is perfectly correct, for example, to regard the sentences of (55) as cognitively identical.

(55a) Já foi inaugurada a ponte?
(55b) Já se inaugurou a ponte?
(56) A ponte já foi inaugurada?
} 'Has the bridge been open to the public?'

There is, however, an important difference between (55a), (55b), and (56) as regards the distribution of information. In (55a), (55b), the noun *ponte* constitutes the focus of the question, that is, its rheme, whereas in (56) this function is attributed to the verb. It is easy to interpret this difference in terms of word order when only passives are involved, as in (55a), which follows the pattern verb + subject, and in (56), where the pattern is subject + verb. As regards (55b), it is worth noticing that the order *se* + verb + object (or verb + *se* + object, as in *Inaugurou-se a ponte*) is far more common than the sequence in which the direct object precedes the group made up by the verb and the pronoun, as in (57).

(57a) A ponte já se inaugurou?
(57b) A ponte inaugurou-se ontem.

An indeterminate actor is necessarily thematic and carries a low degree of CD.[15] In any case, the indeterminate *se* is always unstressed and cannot receive sentence stress. Thus, although a choice is possible between the surface patterns of (58), given the general tendency of the language to place the element with higher communicative dynamism at the end, where it is identified as the rheme, that choice depends on the relative distribution of CD between the NP_{goal} and the group VP + *se*.

(58a) NP_{goal} VP + *se*

(58b) VP + *se* NP_{goal}

The semantic configuration underlying either (55b) or (57), where the goal noun is nonhuman and the verb expresses a human action, cannot yield a truly reflexive sentence. However, if that noun is human, there is room for potential ambiguity, as the patterns of (58) are very similar to constructions in which the pronoun *se* functions as the surface indicator of a reflexive or reciprocal action, rather than as a marker of actor indeterminacy. Such ambiguity is less likely to occur if (58a) is chosen, as in (59), (60), than if (58b) is selected, as in (61), (62).

(59) O candidato matou-se.
'The candidate killed himself.'
(60) Os candidatos mataram-se.
'The candidates killed themselves/each other/one another.'
(61) Matou-se o candidato.
(61a) 'The candidate killed himself.'
(61b) 'The candidate was killed.'
(62) Mataram-se os candidatos.
(62a) 'The candidates killed themselves/each other/one another.'
(62b) 'The candidates were killed.'

In sentences like (61) and (62), by virtue of not being in the normal sentence-initial subject position, the noun phrase may be interpreted either as a rhematic actor (glosses (61a), (62a)), or as a rhematic goal (glosses (61b), (62b)). Nevertheless, the possibility for ambiguity remains, and a common solution, when a plural goal noun is involved, consists in using the indefinite *se* associated with a singular verb, as in (63).

(63) Matou-se os candidatos.
'The candidates were killed.'

Ambiguity does not occur when the noun is inanimate, since in such a case a reflexive action is not possible. Even so, the similarity with reflexive sentences is strong enough that most informants would shun sentences like (57a), (57b) in favor of agentless passives like (56).

There is a class of verbs which cannot appear in truly reflexive sentences since they denote actions an actor cannot perform on himself. These are verbs such as *massacrar* 'to massacre', *fuzilar* 'to execute by a firing squad', *aprisionar* 'to take prisoner', *assassinar* 'to murder', and so on.[16] Thus, if one such verb is used with the indeterminate *se*, the reflexive interpretation is barred. However, my informants have evinced a tendency to reject the use of such verbs in sentences with pattern (58a), even though the only interpretation they would assign to sentences like (64), (65) was that involving the indeterminate *se*. The reason seems to be that the word order in these sentences parallels too closely for comfort that of the unmarked sequence subject-verb-object. On the other hand, if we used pattern (58b), which yields sentences (66), (67), the rhematic status of the verb would have to be indicated by stressing the verb.

(64) O prisioneiro fuzilou-se.
'The prisoner was shot by a firing squad.'
(65) A milionária sequestrou-se.
'The millionairess was kidnapped.'
(66) Fuzilou-se o prisioneiro.
'The prisoner was shot by a firing squad.'
(67) Sequestrou-se a milionária.
'The millionairess was kidnapped.'[17]

This type of contrast is illustrated by sentence (68), as opposed to (69), where capitals indicate contrastive stress, which coincides with sentence stress.

(68) RAPTOU-se a menina.
'The girl was KIDNAPPED.'

(69) RESGATOU-se a menina.
'The girl was RESCUED.'

These limitations on the use of the indeterminate *se* result primarily from the possibility of confusion with reflexive or reciprocal homonymous sentences. Consequently, some functional gaps are created in the cases in which the verb is rhematic, that is, when it carries more CD than the associated NP. A solution for this difficulty is provided by the use of agentless passives. When there is equivalence in FSP between the two sentence types, they can be used interchangeably.

It appears that passive sentences, as opposed to nonpassives, are relatively infrequent in colloquial Brazilian Portuguese. In a corpus containing 81,091 verb forms culled from recordings of conversations on amateur frequencies, Hutchins (1975:61) identified only 3,371 occurrences of the past participle (4.16 percent of the total). Of these, 643 (0.8 percent) cooccurred with *estar* and only 515 (0.6 percent) with *ser*. Even if all cases of *ser* + participle were passive constructions, this last figure would still be rather low. However, when only sentences involving actor indeterminacy are considered, agentless passives appear as a major single device for signalling this phenomenon. In the tape recordings of a series of informal conversations among eight adult Brazilians (in groups of three or four, with a total recorded time of about five hours), I have found that agentless passives accounted for about 25 percent of all actor indeterminacy markers, *a gente* for 17.4 percent, the indeterminate *se* for 17.0 percent, nonspecific *você* for 13.3 percent, deleted *eles* for 13.0 percent, the lexicalized noun phrases *o sujeito* and *o pessoal* for 6.9 percent and 3.4 percent respectively, and explicit *eles* for only 3.0 percent. Agentful passives accounted for less than 2 percent of all passive sentences.

The proportions are somewhat different in informal writing, as shown by the analysis of 106 letters written by 18 Brazilians. In 300 sentences of the types studied here, there were only 6 percent of agentful passives; the remainder included agentless passives (31 percent), the indeterminate *se* (29 percent), *a gente* (22 percent), deleted *eles* (11 percent), and explicit *eles* (1 percent). There were no instances of lexicalized noun phrases such as *o pessoal*, etc., nor of nonspecific *você*.

While these samples are admittedly too small and limited for anything more than speculative generalizations, one can suggest some explanations for the differences between the two corpora. Increased use of actor indeterminacy markers in writing reflects a higher occurrence of those markers least likely to create ambiguity, that is, *a gente* and the indeterminate *se*. Furthermore, while the percentage of incidence of agentless passives remained stable, the use of unspecified *você* dropped to zero, which is not surprising, considering that this pronoun, when used in a letter, is very likely to be interpreted as a term of direct address. The small reduction in the use of deleted *eles* is probably not very significant; the sharp drop in occurrence of explicit *eles* (the three sentences in the written corpus were marginal at best), however, may have been due to a desire to avoid a form which, in writing, stands a good chance of being taken for an anaphoric pronoun. Finally, the disappearance of lexicalized noun phrases like *o sujeito*, etc., seems to reflect the fact that these are typical of spoken registers, as mentioned earlier. Only a large-scale study of the relative functional load of these different types of actor indeterminacy markers in different styles and registers may be able to clarify whether they have any sociolinguistic relevance, that is, whether there are any observable correlations between their rate of occurrence and speaker's variables such as education, social class, and the like.

The actor indeterminacy markers seen in this chapter present the English-speaking learner of Portuguese with a few problems which, while not overwhelming, are nevertheless worthy of attention. Lexicalized noun phrases such as *o cara* and *o sujeito* have structural and functional counterparts in English (see note 3), and the main contrast between the two languages is that while English favors the indefinite article (*a man, a guy*), Portuguese favors the definite article. In either language, the noun is taken in a generic sense and can usually be taken as referring to persons of either sex. If it is important to specify the sex, a generic feminine noun is used in Portuguese, as in (70).

(70) Hoje em dia nos Estados Unidos, se a dona quer abortar, não é mais ilegal. (TRC)
'Nowadays in the United States, if a woman wants to abort, it is no longer illegal.'

Lexicalized noun phrases such as *o cara* function idiomatically and should be learned as wholes, with due attention paid to the fact that they belong to informal registers. If an indefinite article is substituted, yielding *um cara, um sujeito*, generic status is retained, but then what one has is an ordinary, nonlexicalized noun phrase.

The idiom *a gente*[18] is homonymous with the nonlexicalized noun phrase *a gente* 'the people', as in (71).

(71) A gente que mora lá não presta.
'The people who live there are good for nothing.'

This homonym sometimes leads the learner to use *a gente* 'people' in constructions where the lexicalized idiom does not belong, as in (72), and he should therefore be taught to use nonlexicalized noun phrases such as *as pessoas* or *o povo*, or idioms such as *o pessoal* or *a turma*, as in (73).

(72) Hoje em dia a gente não quer mais trabalhar.
[intended meaning: 'Nowadays people do not want to work any longer.']

(73) Hoje em dia as pessoas (o povo/o pessoal/a turma) não querem (quer) mais trabalhar.[19]

Whereas the actor indeterminacy marker *eles* is paralleled by nonspecific *they* in English, deleted *eles* has no counterpart in this language. However, the optional Portuguese rule that allows deletion of the subject is general enough that students who have mastered it in regular constructions usually experience no difficulty in applying it to the case of deleted generic *eles*. This is what they should be encouraged to do, as such deletion is far more common than the use of overt *eles*. It is interesting to notice that overt generic *eles* can be used for emphasizing the nonanaphoric value of its deleted counterpart, as in the following dialogue.

(74) Estão dizendo que o leite vai subir de novo.
'They are saying that the price of milk is going up again.'
Quem é que te disse isso?
'Who told you that?'
Ninguém, não. Eles é que estão dizendo.
'Nobody, really. They [= no one in particular] are the ones who are saying it.'

Except when word order patterns not found in English are involved, passives present few structural difficulties besides the subject-participle agreement in gender and number found in all *ser/estar* + participle constructions. Thus they can be learned with a minimum of difficulty, provided that they are presented as structures in their own right, rather than as transforms of active sentences. Such transformations, so dear to teachers, are clearly an impossibility in the case of agentless passives, unless one resorts to artificial operations such as *Alguém comprou aquela casa* → *Aquela casa foi comprada (alguém* → *∅)*, whose pedagogical value is debatable.

Sentences with the indeterminate *se*, however, are unique enough to require the learner to make a conscious effort to use them at all, and to do so appropriately. They should be taught as separate structures in their own right, and not together with the reflexive pronoun *se*. From a synchronic viewpoint, there is no relationship between sentences like (74a) and (74b).

(74a) Pedro lavou-se.
'Pedro washed himself.'

(74b) Lavou-se o carro.
'One washed the car.'

Teaching constructions like (74b) as involving some special use of the reflexive pronoun serves only to create confusion in the mind of the learner, who quite rightly fails to perceive any reflexive action in them. It is much simpler to start by pointing out the semantic parallel between the indeterminate *se* and the indeterminate pronoun *one* in English, in simple sentences such as (75).

(75) How does one say that in Portuguese?
Como ∅ se diz isso em português?

Agreement between the verb and a plural goal (direct object) noun should be taught as resulting from an alternative interpretation of this noun as the surface subject (though not as the actor). The teacher should be realistic and point out that this agreement is largely optional in the spoken language, and not always adhered to in writing by educated native speakers. Students should also be alerted to the fact that prescriptive grammar insists on agreement, which they should use when writing in consultative or formal style.

NOTES

1. 'The feature that characterizes uniquely the passive construction is the specific type of predicate involved, namely, a perfect participle of a transitive verb' (Câmara 1972:142).

2. '...more properly, of the semantic unit reflected in the surface unit *become*' (Chafe 1970:138).

3. The following diagram serves to illustrate the relations among the three verbs:

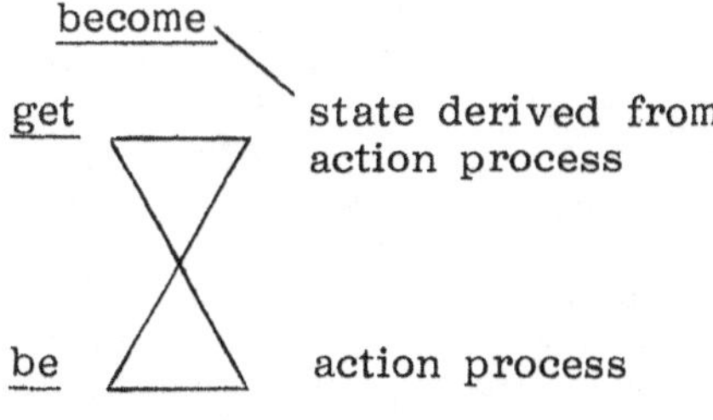

(a) He became frustrated with the delay.
(b) He got frustrated with the delay.
(c) He was frustrated with the delay.
(d) He got frustrated by a policeman.
(e) He was frustrated by a policeman.

The choice of different prepositions by native informants reveals different interpretations. An actor noun phrase which becomes a surface agent is introduced by the preposition *by* (d)-(e), whereas the function causative in examples (a)-(c) is introduced by the preposition *with*. On the related semantic differences, see Svartvik (1966:102f.).

4. *Grow* shares some of the inchoative meaning of *become*, as in *He grew accustomed to the pain*. *Rest* and *stand* seem to occur in more or less stereotyped phrases like those cited by

Jespersen (loc. cit.): *stand condemned*, *stand corrected*, *rest assured*, etc.

5. The difference is not always clear-cut. Ellison et al. (1971:541) follow an old tradition when they state that 'only *ser* is used to form the passive voice. Other verbs meaning *to be* such as *estar*, *ficar*, *andar*, and so on, are never used to form the passive; past participles used with those verbs function as adjectives, and an agent is not expressed'. Bechara (1961:109-110) distinguishes between passives (with *ser*) and sentences with a predicative (i.e. *estar* + participle), although he remarks, in quoting Gili y Gaya (*Curso superior de sintaxis española*, 3rd ed., p. 109), that 'há casos de difícil distinção'.

6. That is, units which 'convert a lexical unit of one type into a lexical unit of another' (Chafe 1970:123).

7. The glosses in this section are approximate semantic equivalents; it is not implied that they are the only or even the best English renderings of the Portuguese sentences given as examples.

8. Like unstressed English *you* /yə/ (see Agard 1970:10), *você* can be nonanaphoric filler. It alternates in this function with its formal counterparts *o senhor, a senhora.*

9. Use of lexicalized noun phrases as actor indeterminacy markers is common to both English and Portuguese, and the same semantic specification shown in (32) applies, regardless of the lexical noun chosen, as in English *a man, a guy, a fellow, a chap*, etc. Besides *o cara,* Portuguese has also *o sujeito, o fulano, o elemento* (Brazilian military lingo), *o gajo* (outdated in Brazil but quite alive in Portugal), and a few others. In very colloquial speech, *os cara* [uskárə] is interchangeable with nonspecific *eles.*

10. The ordering of Almeida's examples in (36) is my own.

11. Almeida's remark on the supposed lack of function of *se* in some of the examples of (36) should be interpreted as a comment on the redundancy of the use of this pronoun with an infinitive. Notice, however, that the presence or absence of *se* can change the meaning slightly in (36g), (36h). In (36g), without the pronoun we would have an ambiguous sentence, i.e. *No momento de estourar a bomba.* One of its interpretations would involve the process verb *estourar* 'burst' with no semantic actor; the other would be the same as the gloss, 'At the moment when someone was going to make the bomb explode'. Use of the indeterminate *se* disambiguates the sentence by making clear that an indeterminate actor is implied. In (36h), the pronoun indicates that *o escrivão* 'the notary' is not necessarily the actor associated with the verb *juntar* 'collect', as would be the case if we had only *Ao juntar as folhas, notou o escrivão a falta de uma.*

12. Naro (1976) uses [-definite] instead of indeterminate, and he postulates, in addition, the features [group interpretation] [third person], [clitic], and [nominative/reflexive] as

necessary to account for *se* sentences in his generative model. He also points out that, according to some scholars, there are cases in which *se* can be specified as feminine.

13. The semantic structure of sentences like those of (53) and (54) should be as follows.

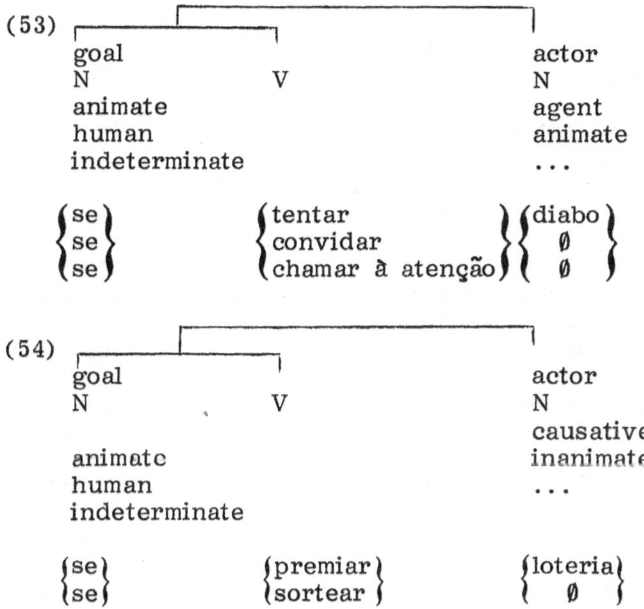

This type of structure represents the only case I know of in which *se* can stand for an element other than the actor in the semantic configuration. In Naro's model (1976:785), there is obligatory passivization, 'or some other transformation that puts *se* in pre-verbal position before clitic placement, because *se* cannot occur in surface object position'.

14. Some scholars who have studied indeterminate *se* sentences in Spanish have attempted to establish a unified treatment which would account not only for sentences like *Se trabajó* 'One worked', and *Se veían las fotos* 'One saw the photos', but also for reflexive constructions such as *Se mató* 'He killed himself', intransitive ones such as *Se quejó* 'He complained', and so on. According to one such analysis (Langacker 1970), one would have to postulate underlying strings like *Juan quejó Juan* and *Las fotos ven las fotos* for the generation of *Juan se quejó* and *Se ven las fotos*; but in my view, this analysis is counterintuitive. (In fact, it was changed in Langacker and Munro 1975; for comments thereon, see Naro 1976.) I do not think any important generalization is lost by keeping the analysis of the indeterminate *se* apart from that of the reflexive *se*; rather, I consider the two *se*'s separate lexical entries, both in

Portuguese and in Spanish, as shown by Lozano, whose articles (1970, 1972) provided the initial stimulus for this study. I have refrained from referring to the rather abundant literature on the indeterminate *se* in Spanish because a comprehensive review of it would require a separate monograph and because I wished to treat the cognate Portuguese construction in its own right.

15. Some of the material in the remainder of this chapter was presented in Azevedo (1976).

16. The distinction between [+reflexizable] and [-reflexizable] verbs does not necessarily hold in figurative language. Thus, we can have, for example, *Ele se sequestrou para obter um resgate* (TRC), meaning 'He pretended to have been kidnapped in order to collect ransom', rather than 'He kidnapped himself'.

17. Notwithstanding the prescriptive rule according to which unstressed pronouns should not occur in sentence-initial position, sentences like *Se fuzilou o prisioneiro* and *Se sequestrou a milionária* are perfectly acceptable alternatives to (66) and (67) in spoken colloquial Brazilian Portuguese.

18. For a detailed analysis of *a gente*, see Schmitz (1973).

19. Although these idiomatic noun phrases have been analyzed here as actor indeterminacy markers, they can also fulfill other syntactic functions, where they retain their indeterminate semantic value, as in (i)-(ii).

(i) Quanto o chefe manda chamar a gente/o cara/o pessoal, o melhor é vir.
'When the boss sends for us/a guy/the guys it is better to come.'

(ii) Se você precisar da gente, é só telefonar.
'If you need us, all you have to do is to call up.'

3

CONTRASTIVE ANALYSIS OF PASSIVE CONSTRUCTIONS

3.1 **Preliminaries.** The contrastive analysis of Portuguese and English passive sentence types presented here represents a compromise between the requirements of autonomous models, as opposed to generalized ones (Di Pietro 1971:18f.). Its statements are made in terms of a direct comparison of surface syntactic structures, which makes possible an economical discussion of the facts. The rationale for this choice is based on the view that passive constructions are the result of post-semantic processes, even though these are determined by phenomena at the semantic level of sentence organization. Passivization functions as a device which creates certain types of linearization of postsemantic elements, according to different possibilities of distribution of information, defined in terms of communicative dynamism, at the semantic level. Since we are interested in how the distribution of CD is reflected in the surface structure, a detailed comparison of how each pattern is generated in each language would be beyond the scope of this analysis. The surface patterns examined below result from the application of rules of primary linearization such as those presented in Chapter One. For some of the patterns, the rules presented there should suffice; for others, additional rules can be formulated without difficulty by the reader.

From a theoretical standpoint, contrastive analysis serves to illuminate similarities and differences between two or more languages. This is certainly not a minor contribution, since comparison of different languages is a means of providing an empirical basis for generalizations about language. However, the pedagogical value of contrastive analysis, once enthusiastically defended (Fries 1945), has been the object of much debate for about a decade or so. Some scholars have voiced strong rejection of one or more of its tenets and techniques (Hadlich 1965, Hamp 1968, Lee 1968, Newmark and Reibel 1968), while others have come to its defense and shown that a good deal of that criticism stemmed from incorrect interpretation of the premises and goals of contrastive linguistics. Particularly hard criticism has been aimed at the so-called 'strong version' of contrastive analysis (Wardhaugh 1970), which claims that it serves to predict learners' errors. However, many critics accept that contrastive analysis can contribute to explaining some errors--at least, those errors that can be traced to contrasts between the languages involved. The experience of foreign language teachers shows that contrast points between source language and target language can constitute troublesome spots for learners, who tend to produce deviant utterances which can be explained as resulting from undue application of source language rules to the production of target language constructions. The present analysis is not committed, one way or another, to the question of error prediction; rather, it is based on the premise that, whatever other variables may be involved, the hypothesis of source language interference remains a useful means of explaining a number of learners' errors, and that a contrastive analysis can provide teachers with the elements for identifying and understanding those errors, as well as for designing exercises for helping students produce the desirable correct sentences.[1]

It is assumed that both in English and Portuguese the semantic structure of sentences contains information regarding the degree of CD ascribed to each constituent. The distribution of CD largely explains the order in which those constituents are represented in the surface structure, so that those with higher CD will be relatively more emphasized than those with less CD. The two languages differ in the specific means they employ to achieve the distribution of CD in terms of theme and rheme, and passivization is one of the resources available to both languages. The fact that Portuguese has a more flexible system of word order rules than English allows it to organize sentence patterns in a variety of ways which either are unavailable in or have more limited use in English.

Taking a common semantic configuration as a point of departure,[2] we arrive at an intermediate, nonlinearized postsemantic structure which undergoes different primary and secondary linearization rules in order to yield one of the possible surface patterns.

The comparison of Portuguese and English passives derived from semantic configurations similar to those used in the sample derivation of Chapter One yields different types of contrasts. Some have to do with postsemantic processes, and are contrasts which hold globally and involve gender and number agreement of the participle with the subject and choice of language-specific prepositions which introduce the agent noun phrase. Other contrasts have to do with different word order arrangements and result from differences between the two systems of primary linearization rules.

Given two surface patterns, such as NP:SJ + VP and VP + NP:SJ, as in *O menino foi morto* and *Foi morto o menino*, respectively, we can say that the rules accounting for the differences between the two patterns have to do with the linearization of the subject NP and its VP in relation to each other. Given normal placement of sentence stress, it can be postulated that in the first sentence VP has higher CD than NP, whereas in the second, the opposite situation obtains. The first sentence can easily be an answer to a question such as *Que aconteceu com o menino?*, whereas the second one would rather answer a question such as *Quem foi morto?* Either sentence can contain entirely new information if used as an answer to, say, *O que aconteceu?*, and choice of one or the other will depend on the speaker's decision as to whether the NP or the VP is rhematic.

Since agentless passives are not derived from agentful ones (except in cases of agent deletion), but rather have a derivational history of their own, surface patterns of both kinds are listed here. Pedagogical comments are made throughout the presentation in order to highlight the sort of difficulties which certain Portuguese patterns present to English-speaking students. The error types presented by way of examples are those which, having been noticed in the classroom and in written compositions, seem susceptible of explanation in terms of interference from English. Other error types, for which such explanation did not seem appropriate, have been left out. Also, instead of treating English and Portuguese patterns separately before proceeding to the contrastive analysis proper, a single treatment has been adopted.[3]

3.2 First set of patterns.

(1) Eng. 1.

a. NP:SJ VP AG
Our house was bought by a realtor (TRC).

b. NP:SJ VP
...when the new French president was inaugurated (TRC).

c. AG NP:SJ VP
By the king a proclamation was issued.

d. AG AuxPas NP:SJ Part
By the Almighty was the kingdom saved.

(2) Ptg. 1.

a. NP:SJ VP AG
'Um operário maoísta...foi abatido pelo serviço de ordem da empresa...' [*Visão*, Oct. 10, 1972, p. 31].

b. NP:SJ VP
'Meu maninho foi operado novamente' [from a letter].

c. VP AG
Foi defendida pelo sangue do povo.

d. VP
Vai ser preso! (TRC)

e. VP NP:SJ AG
Finalmente foi conquistado o último reduto guerrilheiro por tropas do exército e da polícia.

f. VP NP:SJ
'Foi inaugurado...o primeiro sistema de comunicações diretas em ondas curtas entre o Brasil e a Bolívia' [*Boletim Especial* June 7, 1971].

g. VP AG NP:SJ
'Em comemoração à data, foi inaugurado a 3 do corrente, pelo Presidente da República, o Palácio da Justiça' [*Boletim Especial* June 7, 1972].

h. AuxPas NP:SJ Part AG
Por essa razão, foram os alunos suspensos pelo diretor.

i. AuxPas NP:SJ Part
Assim, serão as manadas salvas da enchente.

j. AG NP:SJ VP
Pelo presidente, uma nova represa será inaugurada.

k. AG VP NP:SJ
Pelo presidente, será inaugurada uma nova represa.

l. AG AuxPas NP:SJ Part
Pelo presidente, será uma nova represa inaugurada.

Patterns Ptg. 1(a,b) should not pose any particular difficulty to the learner, since they are structurally identical to their counterparts Eng. 1(a,b). In either language, NP:SJ is usually thematic and can contain new information, as in (3), (4), or old information, as in (5), (6). In the latter case, NP:SJ can be pronominalized. If AG is new, it is specified for a higher degree of CD, and consequently it receives sentence stress, as in (7) and (8). If AG is nonnew, it may be pronominalized, and sentence stress falls on the verb, as in (9) and (10).

(3) [Que aconteceu?]
a. Uma menina foi morta por um louco.
b. Uma menina foi assassinada.

(4) [What happened?]
a. A girl was killed by a madman.
b. A girl was murdered.

(5) [Que aconteceu com o chefe?]
a. Ele foi atropelado por uma lambreta.
b. Ele foi assaltado.

(6) [What happened to the boss?]
a. He was run over by a scooter.
b. He was robbed.

(7) [Que é que a Maria te contou?]
Contou que ela já foi caloteada pelo Paulo Silva.

(8) [What did Mary tell you?]
She told me that she was cheated by Paul Smith.

(9) [Que é que a Maria te contou do Paulo?]
Contou que ela já foi caloteada por ele.

(10) [What did Mary tell you about Paul?]
She told me that she was swindled by him.[4]

Deletion of a nonnew NP:SJ is possible in Portuguese and serves to generate patterns Ptg. 1(c,d), which may occur in contexts in which the deleted NP is retrievable, as in (11).

(11a) [The same NP underlies a series of coordinated sentences.]
A nossa cidade foi fundada por gente do povo; foi defendida pelo sangue do povo; foi desenvolvida pelo trabalho do povo...

(11b) [In dialogues, after NP:SJ has appeared.]
E o teu primo?
Vai ser promovido.

The learning problem involved here is that the optional deletion of NP:SJ has no equivalent in Standard English, except in very informal registers, as in the dialogue: 'What about your cousin?' 'Got promoted last week'. Such patterns of colloquial speech can be capitalized on in the teaching of patterns Ptg. 1(c,d). Furthermore, since deletion of NP:SJ can occur independently of passivization, learners are likely to have already mastered the relevant rules by the time these patterns are presented to them.

Patterns Ptg. 1(e,f,g) occur in contexts where the information content of the verb phrase is outweighed by that of NP:SJ (and also of AG, in the case of Ptg. 1(e)). Consequently, the VP is thematized. The decision as to the relative position of NP:SJ and AG--that is, the choice between Ptg. 1(e) and Ptg. 1(g)--depends on similar factors: the phrase which the speaker regards as containing the higher degree of CD is normally placed last.

Patterns Ptg. 1(h,i) are the product of a primary linearization rule which can be labelled, for lack of a better term, 'VP split', the effect of which consists in placing the NP:SJ between AuxPas and Vpart, as shown in (12).

SJ SJ

(12) VP split: V_2 V_1 N — V_2 N V_1

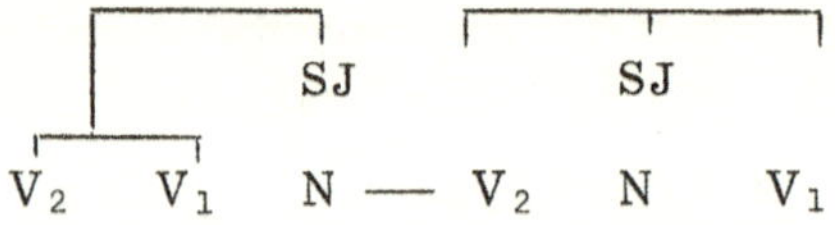

These patterns constitute stylistic possibilities typical of formal registers. Students should learn to recognize them as such, lest they use them on account of the existence of similar patterns in English, which occur in interrogative sentences such as (13).

(13a) Was the building taken by the strikers?
(13b) Were the tenants evicted?

While these English sentences can occur even in very colloquial speech, their Portuguese counterparts are rather more formal.

(14a) Foi o prédio tomado pelos grevistas?
(14b) Foram os moradores expulsos?

The sentences in (15), on the other hand, are more likely to occur in nonformal registers.

(15a) O prédio foi tomado pelos grevistas?
(15b) Os moradores foram expulsos?

The teacher's problem in this case is twofold, as he wants to discourage his learners from associating Ptg. 1(h,i) with interrogative sentences alone and also from using such patterns in ordinary conversation.

Patterns Ptg. 1(j,k,l), as well as Eng. 1(c,d), are characterized by the presence of the agent phrase before all the other elements; they can be considered stylistic variations in which that phrase is thematized rhetorically, so as to become part of a separate intonation contour, as shown in (16).

(16) ^{2}Pelo presi^{3}dente $\left\{ \begin{array}{l} ^{2}\text{uma nova represa será inaugu}^{1}\text{rada.} \\ ^{2}\text{será inaugurada uma nova re}^{1}\text{presa.} \\ ^{2}\text{será uma nova represa inaugu}^{1}\text{rada.} \end{array} \right.$

The existence of Eng. 1(c) (= Ptg. 1(j)) and Eng. 1(d) (= Ptg. 1(l)) should make things easy for the learner, not only because of the structural similarity of the patterns but also because they are all optional and belong to the same (rhetorical and/or poetical) registers in both languages. It is an open question whether the average learner will ever have to use such constructions in Portuguese. On the other hand, the ability to recognize and interpret them is usually achieved without much difficulty.

Postposition of NP:SJ in English can occur under certain circumstances, namely, when certain adverbs are linearized in sentence-initial position (e.g. *Never was a doctor called*). If no such adverb is present, postposition of NP:SJ is often followed by a rule like (17), which introduces a semantically empty root in the position that would otherwise be occupied by NP:SJ, thus originating patterns Eng. 1.1(a,b). If the VP-split rule also applies, we have Eng. 1.1(c,d).

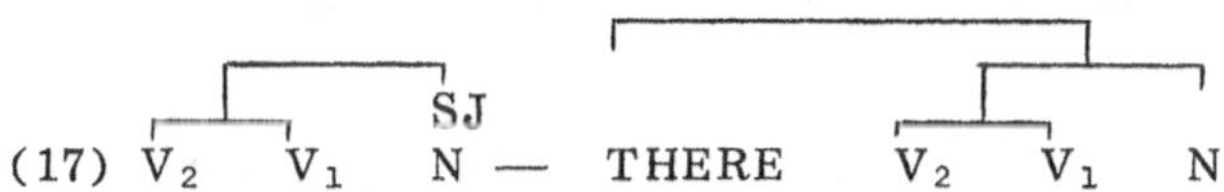

(18) Eng. 1.1

a. THERE VP NP:SJ AG
In old Thule, there was crowned a mighty king by the noblemen.

b. THERE VP NP:SJ AG
Under that fig-tree there was stoned a man...

c. THERE AuxPas NP:SJ AG
'Anything happen at the meeting?'
'Yeah, there was a man killed by the riot cops' (TRC).

d. THERE AuxPas NP:SJ VP
'I hear your house has been robbed. Any big losses?'
'Well, there were a few things stolen and some food spilled on the kitchen floor' (TRC).

Since Portuguese has no structural equivalents of patterns Eng. 1.1, there is no possibility of negative transfer in this case.

Let us now consider a group of patterns which, in spite of differing in important ways from the others seen so far, should be included in this section. For English, they are as follows.

(19) Eng. 1.2
a. NP:SJ VPcomplex AG
b. NP:SJ VPcomplex

The distinctive characteristic of these constructions is the occurrence of complex VPs containing certain invariable elements associated with the verb root and forming surface structures such as those of sentences (20)-(22).

(20a) Holmes was called up by Watson.
(20b) The war was brought about by the technocrats.
(20c) Those records were put away by the butler.

(21a) Phil was laughed at by the students.
(21b) Falstaff was relied upon by Henry.
(21c) Scrooge was called upon by three ghosts.

(22a) For three years, Chris was put up with by the boss.
(22b) Legree was looked down upon by Tom.

(23a) That pool has never been jumped into by a virgin.
(23b) Our house was broken into by burglars last night.

The group VP + invariable particle in (20) stands for a whole semantic unit, and analyses made within different frameworks bear out the view that those groups can be introduced as whole lexical units in the semantic configuration.[5]

The sentences of (21), on the other hand, contain groups made up of a verb root plus a preposition. The differences between such groups and those of (20) are well known and need not be dealt with here; for my purposes it suffices to note that certain verbs must be marked for specific prepositions when associated in the semantic structure with a goal noun specified as a complement of one type or another. It appears that in both English and Portuguese, the choice of a specific preposition depends on the type of complement the goal stands for (Câmara 1972:217f.).

A tentative rule for describing these facts can be stated as in (24). The insertion of the preposition in the surface structure can be accomplished by means of a rule similar to that which linearizes PrepAgt (SL-105, Chapter One), as in (25).

(24a) $\underset{\underline{\text{root}}}{\text{V}} \longrightarrow\!\!\triangleright\!\triangleright \begin{array}{l}\text{V}\\\underline{\text{root}}\\\text{prep x}\end{array} \;/\; \overset{\text{goal}}{\text{N}}$

(24b) $\begin{array}{l}\text{V}\\\underline{\text{root}}\\\text{prep x}\end{array} \longrightarrow\!\!\triangleright\!\triangleright \underset{\underline{\text{root}}}{\text{V}} \quad \text{prep x}$

(25) V prep x —▷ x V
root root

In (22) there is a combination of the two preceding cases, that is, lexical units of the type verb root + invariable particle that are specified for a given preposition. If this analysis is correct, the semantic configuration of sentences (20)-(22) can be exemplified by the diagrams of (26).

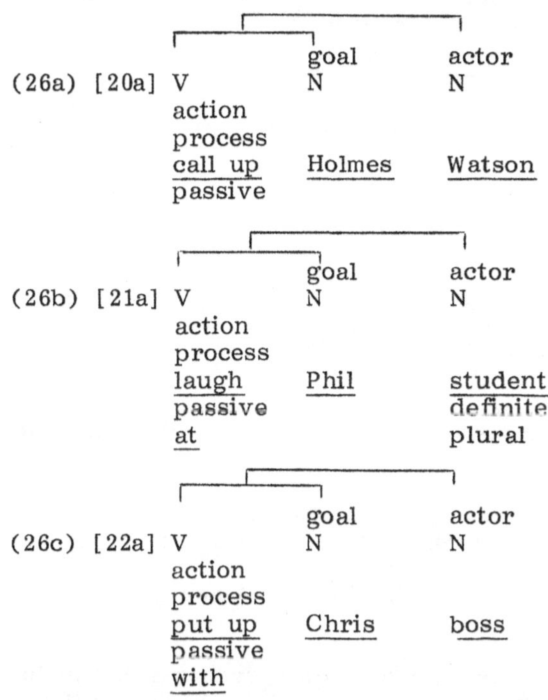

The sentences of (23), however, correspond to more complex semantic structures which contain, associated with the verb root, a locativizer.[6] This is a derivational unit that can be added to a verb to convert it into a locative verb which, in its turn, must be accompanied by a locative (loc) noun. On the other hand, since the verbs of (23) are action verbs as well, they are also associated with actors. The semantic configuration underlying the sentences of (23) can be diagrammed as in (27).

(27) [23a] V loc N actor N
action
locative
jump into pool virgin
passive

Since Portuguese does not have lexical units of the type verb + invariable element, it also lacks semantic configurations like (26a) and (26c). However, it does have verbs of the types exemplified in (21) and (23), as evidenced by the sentences of (28), (29) and their semantic configurations.

(28a) Os alunos riram do professor.
(28b) A pátria confia nos generais.
(28c) Maria gosta de Paulo.
(28d) Joana sonhou com aquelas flores.

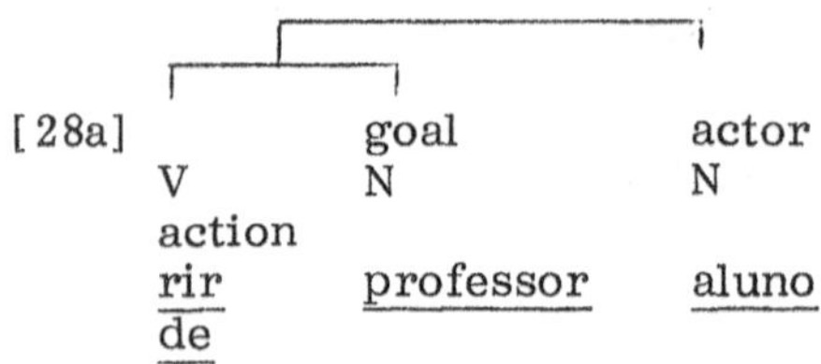

(29a) Uns tatus correram pelo túnel.
(29b) Uma garota pulou na piscina.
(29c) Ele espirrou em mim!
(29d) Entraram ladrões em nossa casa.

(30) Passivization of a root + preposition verb which cannot be passivized, with or without surface realization of the preposition:
a. *O professor foi rido (de) pelos alunos.
b. *Os generais são confiados (em) pela pátria.
c. *Paulo é gostado (de) pelas garotas.
d. *Eu nunca tinha sido latido (para) por um cachorro tão grande.

(31) Passivization of a root + preposition verb which can be passivized, although the realization of the preposition remains ungrammatical:
a. *Essa solução nunca foi sonhada com (por ninguém).
b. Essa solução nunca foi sonhada por(ninguém).

Portuguese 'locativized' action verbs cannot be passivized, hence the ungrammaticality of the sentences of (32), constructed on the basis of their English analogs of (23).

(32a) *Aquela piscina nunca foi pulada (em) por um virgem.
(32b) *Nossa casa foi entrada (em) por ladrões.

3.3 **Second set of patterns.** Let us consider now the semantic configurations of (33), which include, besides a goal and an actor (the latter in (33) only), a beneficiary, which is 'the one who benefits from whatever is communicated by the rest of the sentence' (Chafe 1970:147).[7]

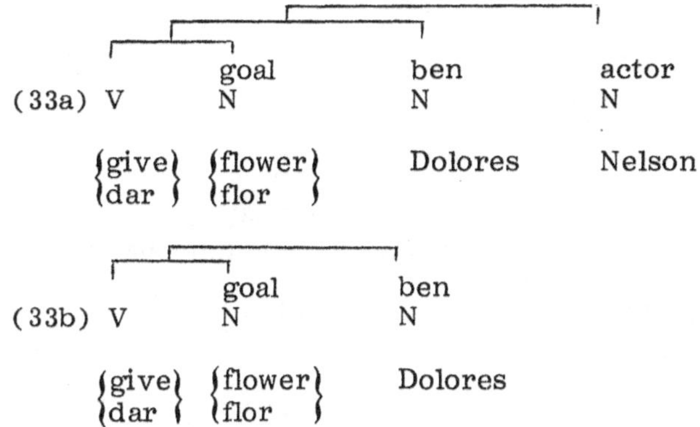

If a noun other than the actor is chosen as the subject in (33a), as must happen in (33b), the verb is passivized. There is an important contrast at this point, namely, that while both the goal and the beneficiary can become the subject in English, only the goal can normally be assigned to that function in Portuguese. This restriction originates two basic types of passive patterns in English, namely, one in which the beneficiary noun appears in the NP:SJ (with the goal noun as direct object) and another in which the goal noun is included in NP:SJ, with the beneficiary in the function of indirect object. In the first case, we would have the following.

(34) Eng. 2.1

a. NPben:SJ VP NPg:DO AG
Dolores was given a flower by Nelson.

b. NPben:SJ VP NPg:DO
Dolores was given a flower.

Given a realization of the full pattern (Eng. 2.1(a)), chances are that AG is rhematic. The constituent NPg:DO is rhematic in Eng. 2.1(b) and probably often in Eng. 2.1(a) as well, unless it is contrastive or contains old information; in the latter case, it may be pronominalized, as in (35).

(35) Anybody that was a little bit failing wasn't told it for fear that he might have a heart attack. (TRC)

If the goal noun becomes the subject, the beneficiary becomes the indirect object. A rule like (36) then applies, associating the indirect object with a preposition (PrepIO) which introduces it in the surface structure. Rule (36) is supplemented by rule (37), which says that PrepIO is optionally deleted if linearized immediately after the verb phrase. If undeleted, PrepIO is eventually replaced by either *to* or *for*, according to rule (38).

```
(36) IO                  ┌──────────┐
                         IO
     N ─────────▷        N           PrepIO
     PRO                 PRO

(37) PrepIO ── ─▷ ∅                  / VP ___

(38) PrepIO ───▷ {to }   / if V is intrinsically benefactive
                 {for}   / if V is accidentally benefactive
```

The following patterns are possible in English.

(39) Eng. 2.2

a. NPg:SJ VP (PrepIO) NPben:IO AG
The flower was given (to) Dolores by Nelson.

b. NPg:SJ VP (PrepIO) NPben:IO AG
The flower was given (to) Dolores.

c. NPg:SJ VP AG PrepIO NPben:IO
The flower was given by Nelson to Dolores.

d. AG AuxPas NPg:SJ Vpart (PrepIO) NPben:IO
By the Almighty was life given (to) Man, that he might enjoy it eternally.

e. To Man was life given, that he might enjoy it eternally.

As regards Portuguese, two sets of patterns are possible, depending on the two different possibilities of pronominalization expressed by the rules of (40), where it is stated that pronominalization of the indirect object can replace it either with a stressed (unmarked) pronoun of the series *mim*, *ti*, *nós*, *ele*, or with an unstressed pronoun of the series *me*, *te*, *nos*, *lhe*. If pronominalization does not take place, or if it does and a stressed pronoun is chosen, a rule like (40c) must apply, replacing that noun or pronoun with a configuration in which this element is associated with PrepIO.

```
       IO          IO
(40a)  N  ── ─▷   PRO

(40b)  PRO ── ─▷ [-stress]

                 ┌──────────────┐
(40c)  IO        IO            PrepIO
       N   ──▷   N
       PRO       PRO
       [+stress]
```

A postsemantic configuration which has been altered by such rules can undergo the application of several different primary linearization rules, which bring about patterns like those in (41).

(41) Ptg. 2.1

a. NPg:SJ VP PrepIO NPben:IO AG
O prêmio foi entregue ao campeão pelo governador.

b. NPg:SJ VP AG PrepIO NPben:IO
O prêmio foi entregue pelo governador aos atletas que chegaram em primeiro lugar.

c. NPg:SJ VP PrepIO NPben:IO
Mais cinco unidades escolares foram entregues à população.

d. VP NPg:SJ PrepIO NPben:IO AG
Foi enviado um novo projeto ao Congresso pelo presidente da República.

e. VP NPg:SJ AG PrepIO NPben:IO
Foi entregue o prêmio pelo presidente aos atletas que representaram o país nas Olimpíadas.

f. VP PrepIO NPben:IO NPg:SJ AG
Foi oferecido aos atletas um jantar comemorativo pelo embaixador do Brasil.

g. VP NPg:SJ PrepIO NPben:IO
Foi entregue o prêmio aos atletas vencedores.

h. PrepIO NPben:IO VP NPg:SJ AG
Ao chefe do governo foi entregue uma carta de protesto pelos chefes sindicalistas.

i. PrepIO NPben:IO VP AG NPg:SJ
'A todas as autoridades do país foi pedida pela Polícia Judiciária a captura de F.A....' [*Diário de Notícias*, Lisbon, 2 June 1972, p. 4].

j. PrepIO NPben:IO VP NPg:SJ
Aos oficiais endividados foi concedido um empréstimo especial de vinte mil dólares.

k. AG NPg:SJ VP PrepIO NPben:IO
Pelo próprio presidente, o decreto da pena de morte foi enviado ao Congresso Nacional para aprovação.

l. AG VP NPg:SJ PrepIO NPben:IO
Pelo próprio presidente, foi enviado o decreto da pena de morte ao Congresso Nacional.

m. AG VP PrepIO NPben:IO NPg:SJ
Pelo próprio presidente, foi enviado ao Congresso Nacional o decreto da pena de morte.

If both (40a) and (40b) apply, since Portuguese unstressed object pronouns are not introduced by prepositions, such pronouns must be linearized either to precede or to follow the finite form of the AuxPas (or the finite form of another auxiliary verb in the case of periphrastic passive constructions such as *O livro lhe tinha sido dado*, in which AuxPas appears in participial form). Besides that, several possibilities of primary linearization exist, and yield the patterns in (42).

(42) Ptg. 2.2

a. NPg:SJ Pro:IO AuxPas Vpart AG
A mensagem lhe foi entregue por um portador especial.

b. NPg:SJ AuxPas Pro:IO Vpart AG
A mensagem foi-lhe entregue por um portador especial.

c. NPg:SJ Pro:IO AuxPas Vpart
A mensagem lhe foi entregue.

d. NPg:SJ AuxPas Pro:IO Vpart
A mensagem foi-lhe entregue.

e. Pro:IO AuxPas Vpart NPg:SJ AG
Quando menos esperava, lhe foi dado um presente pelos amigos.

f. Pro:IO AuxPas Vpart NPg:SJ
Quando menos esperava, lhe foi dado um presente.

g. AuxPas Pro:IO Vpart NPg:SJ AG
Quando menos esperava, foi-lhe dado um presente pelos amigos.

h. AuxPas Pro:IO Vpart NPg:SJ
Quando menos esperava, foi-lhe dado um presente.

i. AG NPg:SJ Pro:IO AuxPas Vpart
Pelos amigos do escritório, um belo presente lhe foi dado no dia de seu aniversário.

j. AG NPg:SJ AuxPas Pro:IO Vpart AG
Pelos amigos do escritório, um belíssimo presente foi-lhe dado no dia de seu aniversário.

k. AG Pro:IO AuxPas Vpart NPg:SJ
Pelos amigos do escritório, lhe foi oferecida uma viagem aos Estados Unidos.

l. AG AuxPas Pro:IO Vpart NPg:SJ
Pelos amigos do escritório, foi-lhe oferecida uma viagem aos Estados Unidos.

One of the problems the teacher has to face, as regards these structures, is the learner's tendency to apply to Portuguese the English rule which allows the assignment of subject function to a beneficiary noun. Students often produce ungrammatical strings such as **Eu fui dado um presente ontem*, **Ela foi dita que não ia ter aula*, etc. This tendency can be eliminated if, in coordination with the first presentation of patterns like those in Ptg. 2.1, the instructor calls the student's attention to the structural difference between the two languages. The explanation can be rendered more meaningful if the learner is made aware of (a) the differences in communicative function between Eng. 2.1 and Eng. 2.2, and (b) the ways in which the same communicative function can be conveyed in Portuguese.

The crucial characteristic of the patterns of Eng. 2.1 is the thematization of the beneficiary noun, which, whether or not it conveys new information, has the lowest degree of CD in the sentence.[8] In patterns Eng. 2(a,b), however, the goal noun appears thematized, and higher degrees of CD are assigned to the actor (if there is one) and the beneficiary.

There are several ways in which the distribution of CD implicit in Eng. 2.1 can be achieved in Portuguese. One of these is the use of an impersonal construction with a subjectless third person plural verb form: *Fizeram-lhe uma proposta que ele não pode recusar.* Another, which interests us more here, is a pattern like Ptg. 2.2(g), that is, *Foi-lhe feita uma proposta que ele não pode recusar.*

The Portuguese patterns of Ptg. 2.1 can be analyzed in terms of CD distribution. In the first three (Ptg. 2.1(a-c)), the subject is thematic. The main difference between Ptg. 2.1(a) and Ptg. 2.1(b) is the relative position of beneficiary and agent. In the latter pattern, the beneficiary carries more CD, understandably since it also contains more information than the agent. Patterns Ptg. 2.1(d-g) represent another type of organization, in which the VP appears as thematic, providing the starting point for what comes next. In Ptg. 2.1(h-j), the theme position is occupied by the beneficiary noun, which carries the highest degree of CD. In Ptg. 2.1(k-m), there is essentially the same situation as in Ptg. 1(j-l), in which the agent is rhetorically thematized and separated from the rest of the sentence by a pause represented in writing by a comma.

Similar considerations apply to the patterns of Ptg. 2.2. Here, however, there is a minor structural contrast in the position of the unstressed indirect object pronoun. While the latter comes after the participle in English, it must come either before or after the AuxPas in nonperiphrastic constructions in Portuguese. This contrast is not specifically linked to passive constructions, although it does pose a certain problem at this level. The instructor's main concern, however, consists in making the students aware of all these possibilities and clarifying the different nuances allowed by those patterns. There is hardly any purpose in trying to enable the learner to use all of the patterns of, say, Ptg. 2.2 at the elementary level of instruction; nevertheless, the ability to identify those patterns as grammatical possibilities and to differentiate between them and ungrammatical ones (e.g. *NPg:SJ AuxPas Vpart Pro:IO) should be developed from the early stages.

3.4 Third set of patterns.

(43a) É sabido pelos ministros que o rei morreu.
(43b) É sabido que o rei morreu.
(43c) It is known by the ministers that the king has died.
(44d) It is known that the king has died.

Semantically, sentences (43a), (43c) are made up of two clauses, the first containing an actor, an experiential verb, and a goal which is itself the second clause. Sentences (43b), (43d) are similar, except that they lack an actor. In a summary way, we can postulate rules (44a), (44b), responsible for the generation of the semantic structures of the sentences of (43), represented in (45).

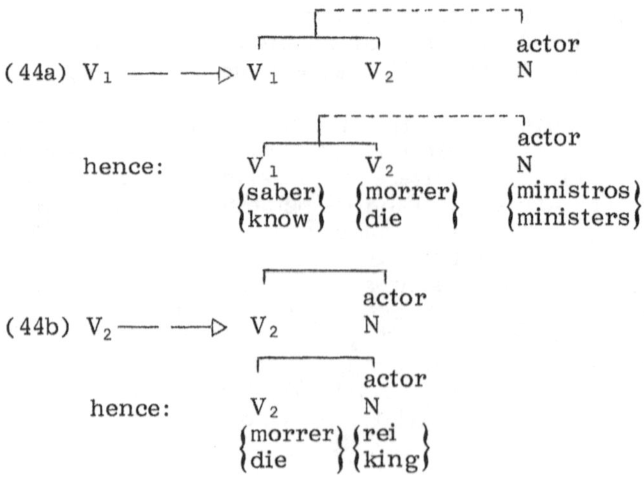

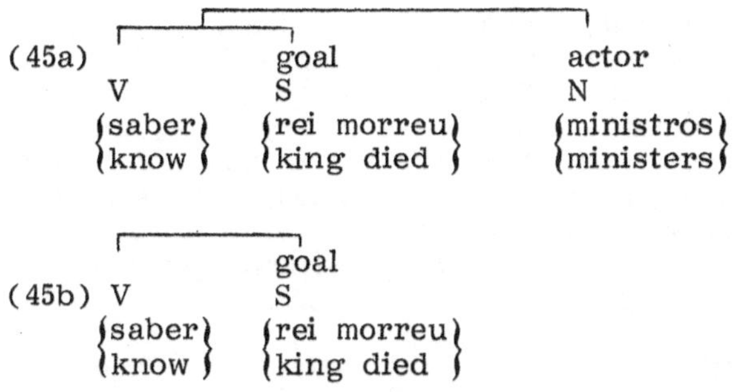

A postsemantic rule inserts a complementizer (Cpl) before the goal sentence, and the choice of the latter as the subject leads to passivization. Different primary linearization rules bring about patterns like those to be described further on. One set of such rules creates the order reflected in Ptg. 3(a,b) and Eng. 3(a,b). In English, the placement of VP in sentence-initial position requires the insertion of the semantically empty pronoun *it*, which occupies the subject position so as to create the order subject-verb, typical of English. As there is no such requirement in Portuguese, the VP stands alone at sentence-initial position. If, however, the actual subject is placed in initial position, we have patterns Ptg. 3(c,d) and Eng. 3(c,d).

(46) Ptg. 3
- a. VP AG Cpl NP:SJ [43a]
- b. VP Cpl NP:SJ [43b]
- c. Cpl NP:SJ VP AG
  Que o rei morreu é sabido pelos ministros.
- d. Cpl NP:SJ VP
  Que o rei morreu é sabido.

(47) Eng. 3
- a. It VP AG Cpl NP:SJ [43c]
- b. It VP Cpl NP:SJ [43d]
- c. Cpl NP:SJ VP AG
  That the king has died is known by the ministers.
- d. Cpl NP:SJ VP
  That the king has died is known.

In both English and Portuguese these different surface arrangements can be interpreted as corresponding to differences in CD distribution. For example, the placement of the VP at the head of the sentences of (43) may indicate that the remaining elements carry a higher degree of CD than the verb, which is thus presented as thematic. In (43a), (43c), the next element, AG, will be rhematic if it contains new information, or it will belong to the theme--or, in an alternate interpretation, to the transition--if it bears already known information. As to the goal, one might expect that, being made up of a whole sentence, it contributes more to the whole message than the passive verb in the main clause. The placement of the subject clause at the end of the sentence serves to emphasize the fact that it carries the most significant part of the message. This is probably an adequate analysis for sentences such as those of (48), in which the subordinated clause is made more complex (and more informative) by the occurrence of multiple embeddings.

(48a) Era sabido por todos que a família real tinha desistido de suas pretensões ao trono, alimentadas durante anos pelo herdeiro presuntivo.
(48b) Foi solicitado que a bandeira do colégio fosse hasteada em sinal de luto pela morte dos estudantes.
(48c) It is required by the university by-laws that all freshmen be in and that lights be out by midnight.
(48d) It was requested that the students start receiving meal tickets valid for the whole week rather than for school days alone.

The interpretation suggested in the preceding paragraphs holds good for the sentences of (43) in case only one intonation contour is present and the sentence stress falls on the last stressed word. A different situation seems to prevail in (49), where the clauses in each sentence have separate intonation contours.

(49a) E' ^{2}sabido^{2} | que o ^{2}rei mor^{1}reu↓

(49b) ^{2}It is ^{3}known^{2} | ^{2}that the king has ^{3}died^{1}↓

In this case, the core of the message is the fact that the king's death is *known* (rather than, say, *surmised*) and the fact that it has occurred carries a lesser degree of CD as regards the sentence as a whole. Once again, word order per se cannot be relied upon exclusively in order to determine the distribution of CD; rather, different possibilities of intonation must be taken into account.

Patterns Ptg. 3(c,d) and Eng. 3(c,d) are generated by the subordinated clause (introduced by the complementizer) in the subject position, followed by the VP and the AG. At first sight, these patterns would apply in a situation diametrically opposed to the one just analyzed, that is, when the subject, even though a complete clause, contains a lesser degree of CD than the remaining elements. Although this is often the case, the preposed subject clause is sometimes set off from the rest of the sentence by means of a separate intonation contour. This results in a pattern which, because of its rheme-theme order, has a rhetorical character, since it presents first (where one would expect to find the theme, i.e. the background information) what is meant to constitute the core of the message. Consider the contrast between the members of the following pairs of sentences.

(50a) Já foi decidido que você não poderá obter a licença.
(50b) Que você não poderá obter a licença, já foi decidido.

(51a) It has already been decided that you will not get a leave.
(51b) That you will not get a leave has already been decided.

The theme-rheme distribution of CD reflected in Ptg. 3(b) is often conveyed by means of a semantic configuration containing an incompletely characterized actor. This actor is realized in the surface structure as the actor indeterminacy marker *se*. Thus, we have both *É sabido que não há água* and *Sabe-se que não há agua; Foi pedido que fizessem silêncio* and *Pediu-se que fizessem silêncio*. With some verbs, speakers of Portuguese often display a marked preference for constructions with AI markers. Thus, we usually find *Solicita-se que venham* rather than *É solicitado que venham; Estranhou-se que não viesse* rather than *Foi estranhado que não viesse*, etc. There is no rule of thumb which may guide the English-speaking student in the choice of the best Portuguese equivalent of an English passive patterned after Eng. 3(a,b); nonetheless, it is advisable to encourage and drill him in the use of sentences with AI markers rather than passives, before introducing him to that problem, the solution of which, in the last instance, is often of a stylistic nature.

3.5 Fourth set of patterns. As a final illustration, let us examine the configuration of (52).

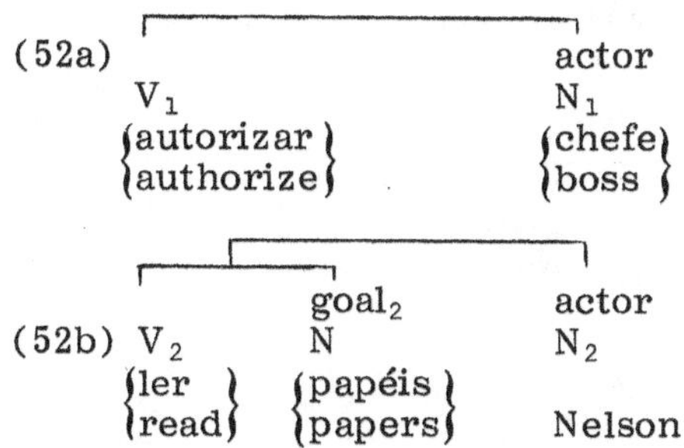

Configuration (52a) is incomplete, in the sense that it cannot generate a grammatical sentence, since its verbs require some sort of complement.[9] However, (52a) and (52b) can combine to form a structure like (53) in which (52a) and (52b) appear, respectively, as the dominant (or superordinate) and the dominated (or subordinate) clauses. Moreover, (52b) now fulfills the role of complement to the verb of (52a).

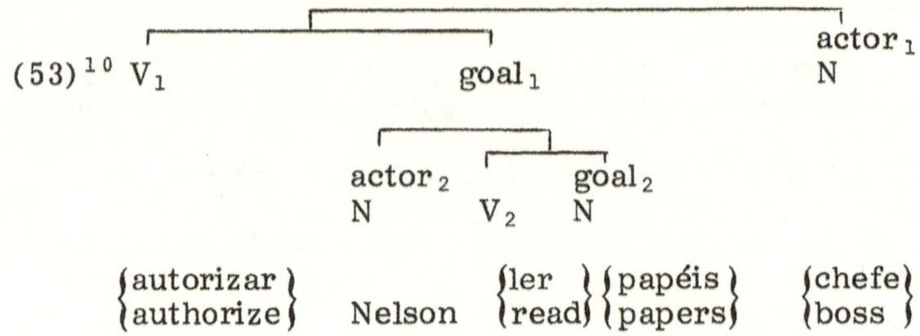

Several different sentences can derive from (52). Since we are interested in passives, let us suppose that the actor$_1$ noun is not chosen as subject (or, alternatively, that there is no such noun in (52) to begin with). Passivization must therefore apply; however, there are different possibilities as to which element will be the subject of the resulting passive sentence.

One possibility is that the dominated goal clause will become the subject, which requires its nominalization; furthermore, the actor$_2$ noun, not having become a subject on account of that nominalization, appears in the nominalized clause as its agent, preceded by PrepAgt. Starting from the diagram in (53), we have the following.

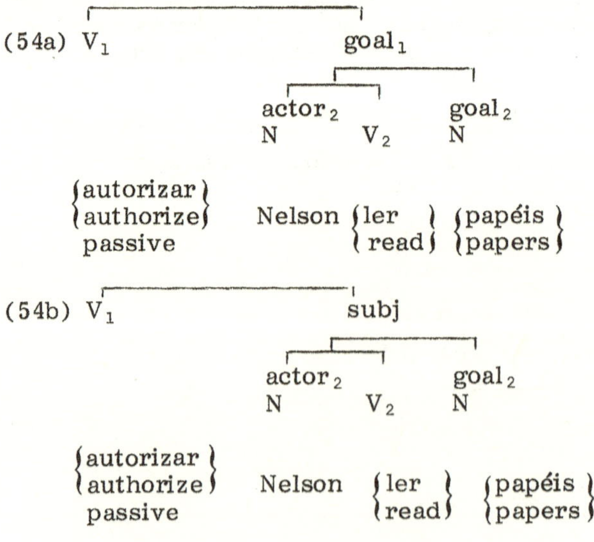

(54c) V_1 subj

S

{autorizar / authorize} {a leitura dos papéis por Nelson / the reading of the papers by Nelson}
passive

Another possibility concerns the choice of $actor_2$ as subject. In this case, the remainder of the dominated clause is removed from its position and linked to V_1. This can be accomplished in different ways, for example, by copying that element onto the superordinate clause and subsequently deleting the 'original' copy by means of an equi-NP deletion transformation. The remainder of the subordinate clause thus remains embedded in the new subject and eventually surfaces as a dependent clause introduced by a preposition: *Nelson foi autorizado a ler os papéis* = *Nelson was authorized to read the papers.* The diagrams in (55) illustrate this derivation.

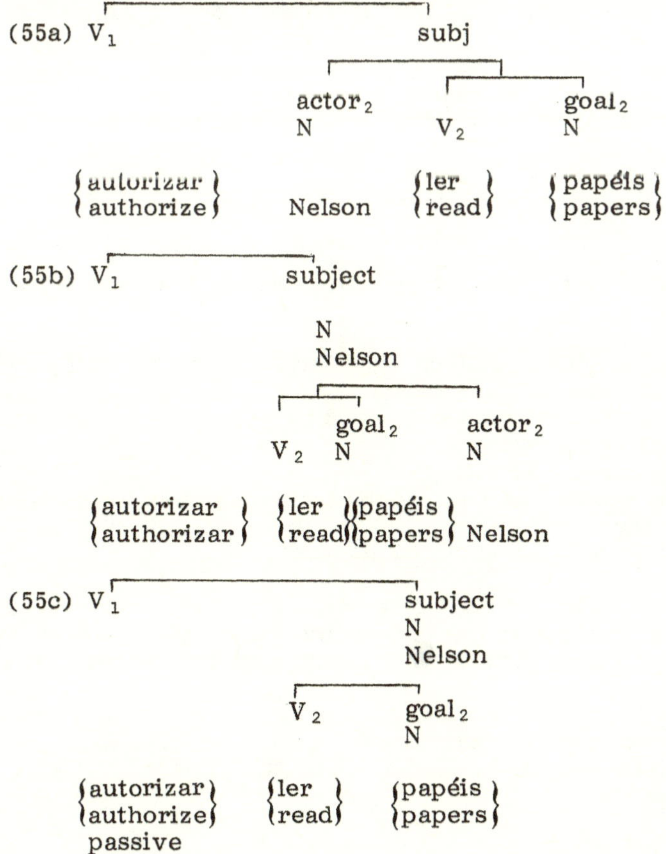

The possibilities just examined yield Portuguese passive patterns which can be described in notational form as follows.

(56) Ptg. 4.1

a. NP Nom:SJ VP AG
A leitura dos papéis por Nelson foi autorizada pelo chefe.

b. AG NP Nom:SJ
Foi autorizada pelo chefe a leitura dos papéis por Nelson.

c. AG VP NP Nom:SJ
Pelo próprio chefe foi autorizada a leitura dos papéis por Nelson.

d. NP Nom:SJ VP
A leitura dos papéis por Nelson foi autorizada.

e. VP NP Nom:SJ
Foi autorizada a leitura dos papéis por Nelson.

(57) Ptg. 4.2

a. NP act_2:SJ VP Prep S AG
Nelson foi autorizado a ler os papéis pelo chefe.

b. NP act_2:SJ VP Prep S
Nelson foi autorizado a ler os papéis.

c. AG VP NP Nom:SJ
Pelo diretor, foi autorizada a leitura dos papéis por Nelson.

The following English patterns also derive from the configurations just examined.

(58) Eng. 4.1

a. NP Nom:SJ VP AG
The reading of the papers by Nelson was authorized by the boss.
Nelson's reading of the papers...

b. NP Nom:SJ VP
The reading of the papers by Nelson was authorized.
Nelson's reading of the papers was authorized...

(59) Eng. 4.2

a. NP act_2:SJ VP Prep S AG
Nelson was authorized to read the papers by the boss.

b. NP act$_2$:SJ VP Prep S
Nelson was authorized to read the papers.

Patterns Ptg. 4.2(a,b) and Eng. 4.2(a,b) are not totally equivalent. Rather, they involve an important contrast which derives from the fact that certain Portuguese verbs, but not others, can occur in Ptg. 4.2(a,b). Thus, for instance, we can have (60) but not (61).

(60) Nelson foi { autorizado / intimado / forçado / obrigado / solicitado } a ler os papéis.

(61) *Nelson foi { permitido / ordenado / exigido / requerido / pedido } a ler os papéis.

Semantically, the verbs in (60) are so close to those in (61) that it would be awkward to distinguish between them on the basis of semantic specifications. *Autorizar* and *permitir*, for example, are synonymous or very nearly so.

The unacceptability of the constructions in (61) is best accounted for as resulting from an idiosyncratic property of verbs such as *permitir, pedir, ordenar*, etc. The learning problem in this case is not structure, since both languages allow the same pattern, namely, Ptg. 4 and Eng. 4. Rather, it is a matter of knowing which Portuguese verbs can occur in Ptg. 4.2(a,b) and which cannot. Usually, verbs which take a dative third person pronoun (*lhe*) do not occur in those patterns, as illustrated by the sentences in (62).[11]

(62a) O juiz requereu-lhe que pagasse a dívida.
(62b) *Ele foi requerido a pagar a dívida pelo juiz.
(62c) Rogaram-lhe que pagasse a dívida.
(62d) *Foi rogado a pagar a dívida.
(62e) Mandou-lhes que pagassem a dívida.
(62f) *Foram mandados a pagar a dívida.

There are, however, exceptions to that rule, such as *solicitar* 'request' and *perguntar* 'query', which, in spite of taking the dative pronoun, do occur in passives such as (63).

(63a) O ministro foi solicitado pelos repórteres a revelar o conteúdo do projeto.
(63b) O presidente foi perguntado sobre a restauração da democracia.

The restrictions which apply to the verbs in (47) and (48) do not have a counterpart in English. Perhaps as a consequence, speakers of this language learning Portuguese often construct nonsentences such as those of (61) and (62b), (62d), (62f), probably misled by the semantic near-equivalence of those verbs and English verbs such as *ask, beg, recommend, command, order*, etc. A practical way to correct this tendency is to teach verbs that behave like those in (60) and (61) as two separate classes which share certain passive patterns but not others.

There is no special reason, other than historical coincidence, why only certain verbs are allowed to occur in patterns Ptg. 4.2. Such discrepant behavior can be related to the matter of whether the third person pronoun that can be associated with the verb in a nonpassive is a dative (*lhe*) or an accusative (*o*) --a distinction which cannot be made for first and second person pronouns. By and large, dative objects do not appear as subjects of passive sentences in Portuguese. The distinction between dative and accusative, however, already reduced to the pronominal forms just mentioned, is blurred in certain varieties of spoken Brazilian Portuguese. Consider the sentences *Eu lhe vi, Depois eu quero lhe ouvir*, which often coexist with or entirely replace the standard variants *Eu o vi, Depois eu quero ouvi-lo*. The restriction which bars constructions like those of (61) seems to be tenuous--that is, it represents a low-level rule attached to certain lexical units.

It is worth noticing that familiarity with English constructions such as *I was asked (requested, ordered*, etc. *)* + *to* + Vinf seems to lead native speakers of Portuguese to produce sentences like those of (61) and (62b), (62d), (62f). For instance, my notes include utterances such as *Eu fui pedido para comparecer no tribunal, Ele foi requerido para pagar o aluguel antecipado*, all produced in ordinary conversation by Brazilian graduate students in the United States. It is well known that prolonged exposure to and use of a foreign language can lead one to incorporate rules of that language into his own. It appears that such incorporation often takes place in points of 'least resistance' in the system. In the present case, the change would consist solely in dropping a certain low-level restriction, thereby allowing certain types of verbs to participate in existing patterns from which they were previously barred. It is curious that the infinitive-introducing preposition used in all such novel sentences should be *para* rather than *a*; this is precisely the same error made by English-speaking students of Portuguese--**Ele foi forçado para confessar o crime*, etc.--probably as a consequence of the partial correspondence between English *to* and Portuguese *para* (as in, for example, *He got up to speak = Ele se levantou para falar*, etc.). Perhaps the findings of contrastive analysis can be profitably used to investigate such phenomena of negative transfer from the target language to the source language.

As mentioned earlier, different possibilities of Portuguese word order, which are a consequence of alternate primary linearization rules, allow the occurrence of other patterns besides those listed. As in the preceding section in this chapter, such alternatives can be interpreted as fulfilling different modes of CD distribution. Let us compare some of those patterns.

In Ptg. 4.1(a), something is predicated of NP Nom:SJ, thus attributing to this element a thematic character. There is also a certain probability that NP Nom:SJ contains old information in a number of cases, since it is specified as definite. The VP is transitional and belongs either to the theme or to the rheme.[12] The AG, which receives sentence stress, is thematic.

In Ptg. 4.1(b), VP is thematic, as it sets the framework for what constitutes the core of the message; as mentioned before, this type of construction, rather common in news items, serves to introduce entirely new information. AG is transitional, and may belong to either theme or rheme. In the latter case it contains a higher degree of CD than in the former, and it may appear set off by internal junctures (indicated by commas as pauses in ordinary writing). The decision as to the thematic or rhematic character of AG, in this and in similar patterns, is often dependent on the degree to which it can be predicted from what is expressed in the VP. In a sentence like (64), there is nothing special about the identity of the agent, since one expects that authorization for work in a museum should be given by its director; in (65), however, there is a high degree of unpredictability as to the identity of the agent.

(64) Foi autorizada pelo diretor do museu a reclassificação dos arquivos.

(65) Foi autorizada, pelo imperador, a limpeza das latrinas do palácio.

Pattern Ptg. 4.1(c) is also of the type that introduces totally new information. The element AG is set off from the remainder of the sentence by a separate intonation contour--as we have already seen, for example, in Ptg. 1(j-1). The distribution of CD in the remainder of the sentence is the same as in Ptg. 4.1(b).

Similar considerations apply to the remaining possibilities listed in this section. The teacher's problem here consists in making his students aware that these patterns are not in free distribution, but rather that they serve to express important nuances in communicative intent. This can be facilitated by means of materials employing carefully constructed dialogue situations in which the contrast between patterns can be highlighted. At more advanced levels of instruction, selected examples from literary or nonliterary prose can also be utilized.

The problems involved in learning the sentence types analyzed in this study have to do with matters of structure and of usage. The former include the acquisition of the ability to generate grammatical passives, which means that the learner must internalize a certain number of rules, without necessarily being conscious of their abstract details nor able to verbalize about them. The latter involve the acquisition of the ability to decide when to use a passive construction rather than a nonpassive.

Certain structural contrasts between English and Portuguese constructions of the type AuxPas + Vpart involve agreement rules which apply elsewhere in the latter language, as mentioned earlier in this chapter. While subject agreement presents relatively little difficulty, mastering the rules of agreement between the subject and the participle is sometimes complicated, it seems, by apparent confusion between passives and structures such as (66).

(66) *ter*Aux + Vpart: As aulas tem terminado cedo.
'The classes have been ending early.'

(67) AuxPas + Vpart: As aulas foram encerradas cedo.
'The classes were ended early.'

In (66) there is no agreement between the subject and Vpart, whereas in (67) agreement in gender and number is obligatory between the subject and Vpart. Typical errors include failure to apply either agreement rule or both rules, and they include ungrammatical sequences like those of (68).

(68a) *A peça foi terminado cedo.
(68b) *As peças foram terminado cedo.
(68c) *As peças foram terminados cedo.
(68d) *As peças foram terminada cedo.

A possible starting-point for preventing or correcting such errors is found in exercises involving overt contrasts between the structures represented in (66) and (67). These procedures highlight the lexical difference between the auxiliaries *ter* and *ser*, which serves as a clue for the application or nonapplication of the agreement rules. The ultimate goal is the automatic association of AuxPas with these rules, so as to cover occurrences of *ter* + AuxPas + Vpart, as in (69).

(69a) As aulas tem sido encerradas cedo.
'Classes have been ended early.'
(69b) Os bares tem sido fechados cedo.
'Bars have been closed early.'

Learning can be reinforced through a comparison of (66) and (70), both of which follow the same agreement rules and include the same verbs as possible realizations of either AuxPas or the copula, as shown in (71).

(70) Copula + Vpart.[13]

(71a) Essa moça foi detida pela polícia civil.
'This girl was detained by the civilian police.'
(71b) Essa moça esteve detida pela polícia civil.
'This girl was detained by the civilian police.'

(72a) Essa moça é reservada.
'This girl is a private person.'
(72b) Essa moça está reservada hoje.
'This girl is acting in a private manner today.'

Three types of options have been recognized in contrastive studies (Stockwell, Bowen, and Martin 1965) as regards the contrasts obtaining between two languages. These are: (1) no choice (Ø), when a given pattern does not exist in one of the two languages; (2) optional choice (OP), when rules for generating a given pattern exist in one of the languages, but need not be applied; and (3) obligatory choice (OB), when certain rules exist and must be applied.

In general terms, passivization is optional in both languages, in the sense that speakers are never under any constraint to generate a passive sentence. However, assuming the speaker's choice to do so, let us take as point of departure postsemantic structures at the point of assignment of a noun other than the actor to the function of subject. The relevant contrasts can be arranged along a hierarchy of structural divergence[14] based on the three options listed in the foregoing paragraph, based on the premise that the most difficult target language structures to learn are often those which do not have a counterpart in the source language. Next are those which, although they exist in both languages, differ as to their obligatory vs. optional status; then there are those which exist only in the target language; and finally, there are those which are common to the two languages and match each other as regards their obligatory or optional character. These different relations are summarized in Table 1, adapted from Stockwell, Bowen, and Martin (1965: 283).

There follows a comparison of the patterns I have presented here, together with a few comments on learners' difficulties.

Group 1:
(1) Eng. Ø: Ptg. OB
(a) Occurrence of VP in sentence-initial position when NP:SJ has been complementized and linearized to follow the main clause [Ptg. 3(a,b)].

Table 1. Hierarchy of structural divergence.

Group	Degree of structural divergence	English	Portuguese
1	1	∅	OB
	2	∅	OP
2	3	OP	OB
	4	OB	OP
3	5	OB	∅
	6	OP	∅
4	7	OP	OP
	8	OB	OB

Students occasionally insert a third person singular pronoun *ele*, probably to match the obligatory *it* of Eng. 3(a,b), as in **Ele era sabido que ia ter problemas*. Since this error results from failure to apply the general rule which allows the occurrence of a VP in sentence-initial position, unaccompanied by a subject pronoun, it can be prevented by previous drill of that rule in simpler patterns, such as Ptg. 1(a,e,f,g).

(b) Linearization of unstressed NPpron:IO before or after AuxPas [Ptg. 2.2].

Placement of NPpron:IO after Vpart can be corrected with drills emphasizing the rule that restricts that position to stressed indirect objects introduced by a preposition. Substitution exercises can be designed which alternate two possibilities of unstressed indirect object pronoun placement, as shown in the following dialogues:

(73) [Quando os livros foram dados a ele?]
a'. Os livros lhe foram dados ontem.
a''. Os livros foram-lhe dados ontem.

(74) [O emprego foi oferecido a você por quem?]
a'. O emprego me foi oferecido pelo gerente.
a''. O emprego foi-me oferecido pelo gerente.

(2) Eng., ∅: Ptg. OP.

(a) Deletion of NP:SJ [Ptg. 1(c,d)]. No specific error due to negative transfer seems likely, but students often fail to make use of this deletion rule. Substitution drills followed by cued question-and-answer exercises such as the following facilitate learning the relevant rules.

(75) E o seu primo? [cue: promovido]
Foi promovido.

(76) E esses livros? [cue: comprados em São Paulo]
Foram comprados em São Paulo.

(b) Inversion of NP:SJ and VP, so that the latter appears in sentence-initial position [Ptg. 1(e,f,g)].

For learners who fail to master this possibility, inversion exercises such as the following are useful.

(77) Um cadáver foi encontrado no parque → Foi encontrado um cadáver no parque.

(78) Dez universidades foram inauguradas em São Paulo → Foram inauguradas dez universidades em São Paulo.

Group 2:

(1) Eng. OP: Ptg. OB.

PrepIO is optional in English in the environment /Vpart___NP: IO, but it is obligatory in Portuguese if NP:IO is either a nominal or a stressed pronoun. Typical errors include constructions like **O presente foi dado Paulo, A licença para a festa foi pedida o prefeito*, and so on. The use of a preposition before a nominal indirect object can be practiced and reinforced by means of exercises like those in (79) and (80).

(79) O emprego foi oferecido. [cue: Paulo] → O emprego foi oferecido a Paulo.

(80) Os documentos foram apresentados [cue: o juiz] → Os documentos foram apresentados ao juiz.

Question-and-answer exercises are also useful.

(81) A quem foi oferecido o emprego? [cue: o Paulo]
Foi oferecido ao Paulo.

(82) A quem foram apresentados os documentos? [cue: o juiz]
Foram apresentados ao juiz.

(2) Eng. OP: Ptg. OP. There are no occurrences of this case in the material analyzed for this study.

Group 3:

(1) Eng. OB: Ptg. ∅

(a) If a complex VP is passivized, the verbal participle-preposition is maintained and linearized to follow Vpart. No such possibility exists in Portuguese, since prepositional verbs do not passivize [Eng. 1.2]. Typical errors consist in passivizing a prepositional verb and keeping the preposition in the passive construction.

(b) A semantically empty morpheme (*it*) must be inserted when the S:SJ has been complementized and linearized to follow the main clause [Eng. 3(a,b)]. Possible errors are of the type described in Group 1, (1)(a).

(2) Eng. OP: Ptg. Ø

(a) There is possibility of choice between a goal noun and a beneficiary noun for subject in English. Only the goal noun can be the subject in Portuguese. Typical errors include sequences like **Eu fui oferecido um emprego*, **Ela foi dada um automóvel novo*, and so on. Correction can be achieved by means of exercises requiring the use of unstressed indirect object pronouns: *Foi-me oferecido um emprego*, *Foi-lhe dado um automóvel novo*, and so on.

(b) Inversion of NP:SJ and VP, followed by obligatory insertion of an empty morpheme (*there*) in the subject position [Eng. 1.1]. There is no likelihood of negative transfer into Portuguese, given the absence of a structural equivalent of *there*.

(c) Passivization of certain verbs is ungrammatical in Portuguese, while the English translational (sometimes cognate) equivalents can be passivized [Ptg. 4.2: Eng. 4.2]. Verbs that do not passivize have to be learned individually.

Group 4:

(1) Eng. OP: Ptg. OP

(a) Placement of AG at the head of the sentence, thematizing it rhetorically [e.1(c,d): Ptg. 1(j-l)]. This construction seems to be more rhetorical in English than in Portuguese, but learning it presents no special difficulties. The following cases do not lend themselves to negative transfer.

(b) 'VP split' rule [Ptg. 1(h,i)] is optional in English yes-or-no questions and optional in Portuguese passives. Some learners tend to overuse it in questions, but this is a minor stylistic problem.

(c) Placement of complementized S:SJ in sentence-initial position [Ptg. 3(c,d): Eng. 3(c,d)].

(d) Placement of PrepIO - NPben:IO in sentence-initial position [Ptg. 2.1(h,i,j): Eng. 2.2(e)]. Notice that this construction in English necessitates the application of the 'VP split' rule.

(2) Eng. OB: Ptg. OB

PrepIO is obligatory in English and in Portuguese when the indirect object comes after the agent [Eng. 2.2(c): Ptg. 2.1(c)].

NOTES

1. 'The interference in performance in L_2 target language which can be associated with competence in L_1 source language can be counteracted by exercises which are specially designed to reduce the influence of competence of L_1 on performance in L_2' (Politzer 1972:90).

2. This is not to say that both languages have, in some absolute way, the same semantic structure. Contrastive analysis is only possible, however, if we assume a common basis of

shared features for the languages one wants to analyze (Agard 1970: 3, Di Pietro 1971: 3-4).

3. This approach follows, for the same reasons, the precedent set by Agard and Di Pietro (1965: 2).

4. It goes without saying that the speaker may choose a nonpassive construction which will preserve the same distribution of CD. Thus, the replies to the questions in (9) and (10) might be, respectively, *Contou que ele já a caloteou* and *She told me that he cheated her.* The present analysis is not intended to predict what a speaker would say, but rather to interpret the passive constructions which he might choose to use.

5. For instance, in Stageberg's structuralist analysis (1971: 107), such groups are described as belonging 'to a special class of two-part verbs--like *keep on* (continue), *take off* (depart), *butt in* (interrupt), and *show up* (appear)--that speakers of English seem to sense as single words. A not much different view, based on transformational-generative principles, is put forth by Jacobs and Rosenbaum (1968: 102f.), who characterize those invariable elements as 'verb particles' which 'appear in the deep structure...as features on the verbal segments' and which are introduced into the structure of the sentence by a 'particle segment transformation'.

6. 'Locativizer is...a class of units, any one of which will perform the same locativizing function. This class consists apparently of the various locative states, those verb roots... usually thought of as prepositions. Such verbs...may occur as derivational units attached to nonlocative verb roots...the result in the latter case is a derived verb root which is locative, and which is therefore subject to the accompaniment of a location noun' (Chafe 1970: 162).

7. A distinction should be made between verbs like *give, send, teach, lend,* and others which intrinsically require a beneficiary complement, and others like *build, buy,* and *find,* which may optionally be accompanied by such a complement. Verbs of the former type participate more easily in constructions of the type *John was given a job at the store,* where the beneficiary appears as the subject. In such cases, if the beneficiary becomes the indirect object, it can be preceded by the preposition *to.* Verbs of the latter type, which might be called 'accidentally benefactive', usually do not take a beneficiary noun as their subject, as indicated by the fact that sentences like *I was bought a winter coat by my mother, The princess was made a new pair of shoes,* and others like these, were rejected by some informants, but accepted (sometimes hesitantly) by others. If the beneficiary of such a verb is realized as an indirect object, it can be preceded by the preposition *for*: *A winter coat was bought for me by my mother.*

8. This is true in the ordinary cases of placement of sentence stress on the last stressed syllable. Sentence (i), for

example, conveys a different distribution of CD than sentence (ii), as indicated by differences in sentence stress placement.

(i) ^{2}Bertrand ^{2}Russell was ^{2}awarded a ^{2}Nobel ^{2}Prize for ^{3}literature^1.

(ii) ^{2}Bertrand ^{4}Russell was ^{2}awarded a ^{2}Nobel ^{2}Prize for ^{2}literature^1.

In (ii), however, the gist of the message is the contrast between *Bertrand Russell* and any other possible candidate for the prize. The resulting sentence is contrastive, and consequently, outside the scope of this study.

9. The sentence *O chefe autorizou* should be interpreted as deriving through deletion of an element which would otherwise be the surface object direct. **The boss authorized*, of course, is not an English sentence.

10. Subscript numerals are used for ease of reference only.

11. Example (62f) is correct in the sense of 'They were sent to pay the debt'; in this case, however, *mandar* requires a direct object and the nonpassive equivalent would be *Mandou-os (a) pagar a dívida.* The two instances of *mandar* are separate lexical items.

12. One would only know for sure if the sample sentence were inserted into a broader context. If it were intended as an answer to *Quem autorizou a leitura dos papéis por Nelson?*, it would be within the sphere of the theme. Otherwise, if it were meant as an answer to a query such as, *E a leitura dos papéis por Nelson, em que ficou?*, then it should be interpreted as containing new information and as belonging to the rheme.

13. In (70), the morphological Vpart has adjectival function, but this does not interfere with the pedagogical usefulness of the proposed comparison.

14. I speak of 'structural divergence', rather than of 'hierarchical difficulty' (Stockwell, Bowen, and Martin 1965:283), because the latter expression seems to imply a degree of certainty about what constitutes difficulty for the learner that cannot be supported on the basis of contrastive analysis alone, which does not provide the information needed on the psychological factors involved in foreign language learning in order to substantiate claims about the relative difficulty posed by constructions such as those studied here. I have chosen a terminology which seems more compatible with the subject matter of this chapter.

REFERENCES

The references include, besides those works cited in the text, a few others which have been used for background information.

Agard, Frederick B. 1970. Prelegeri de analiză contrastivă. Centrul de multiplicare al Universității din București.

Agard, Frederick B., and Robert J. Di Pietro. 1965. The grammatical structures of English and Italian. Chicago: The University of Chicago Press.

Alatis, James E., ed. 1968. Georgetown University Round Table on Languages and Linguistics 1968. Washington, D.C.: Georgetown University Press.

Ali, Manoel Said. 1966. Dificuldades da língua portuguesa. Estudos e observações. 6th ed. Rio de Janeiro: Livraria Acadêmica.

Almeida, Napoleão Mendes de. 1967. Gramática metódica da língua portuguesa. São Paulo: Edição Saraiva.

Amaral, Vasco Botelho de. 1947. Glossário crítico de dificuldades do idioma português. Porto: Livraria Simões Lopes.

Azevedo, Milton M. 1973. On passive sentences in English and Portuguese. Ph.D. dissertation. Cornell University. Ithaca, N.Y.: Latin American Studies Center, Cornell University, Dissertation Series No. 54. Mimeo.

Azevedo, Milton M. 1974. On the semantics of *estar* + participle sentences in Portuguese. Linguistics 135.25-33.

Azevedo, Milton M. 1976. Thematic meaning, word order, and indefinite actor sentences in Portuguese. In: Georgetown University Round Table on Languages and Linguistics 1976. Edited by Cléa Rameh. Washington, D.C.: Georgetown University Press. 216-235.

Bechara, Evanildo. 1961. Licões de português. 2nd ed. Rio de Janeiro: Editora Fundo de Cultura.

Boletim Especial. Washington, D.C.: Brazilian Embassy.

Bolinger, Dwight L. 1949. Intonation and analysis. Word 5.248-254.

Bolinger, Dwight L. 1950. Retained objects in Spanish. Hispania 33.237-239.
Bolinger, Dwight L. 1952. Linear modification. Publications of the Modern Language Association 52.1117-1144.
Bolinger, Dwight L. 1954. English prosodic stress and Spanish sentence order. Hispania 37.152-156.
Bolinger, Dwight L. 1961. Syntactic blends and other matters. Language 37.366-381.
Bolinger, Dwight L. 1965. The atomization of meaning. Lg. 41.555-573.
Bolinger, Dwight L. 1972. Accent is predictable (if you're a mind-reader). Lg. 48.633-644.
Bos, Gijsbertha F. 1971. Ambiguity, the opposition active-passive and Chomsky's deep structure. Travaux linguistiques de Prague 4.189-204.
Brandão, Cláudio. 1963. Sintaxe clássica portuguêsa. Belo Horizonte: Imprensa da Universidade de Minas Gerais.
Bueno, Francisco da Silveira. 1944. Gramática normativa da língua portuguesa. Curso superior. São Paulo: Edição Saraiva.
Byrne, D. 1966. Teaching the passive. English language teaching 20.127-130.
Câmara, Joaquim Mattoso, Jr. 1972. The Portuguese language. Translated by Anthony J. Naro. Chicago: The University of Chicago Press.
Cattell, N. R. 1969. The new English grammar: A descriptive introduction. 2nd ed. Cambridge, Mass.: The MIT Press.
Chafe, Wallace L. 1967. Language as symbolization. Lg. 43.57-91.
Chafe, Wallace L. 1968. Idiomaticity as an anomaly in the Chomskyan paradigm. Foundations of Language 4.109-127.
Chafe, Wallace L. 1970. Meaning and the structure of language. Chicago: The University of Chicago Press.
Charleston, Britta M. 1960. Studies on the emotional and affective means of expression in modern English. Swiss Studies in English 46. Bern: Francke Verlag.
Chomsky, Noam. 1957. Syntactic structures. The Hague: Mouton.
Chomsky, Noam. 1965. Aspects of the theory of syntax. Cambridge, Mass.: The MIT Press.
Cinque, Guglielmo. 1976. Appropriateness conditions for the use of passives and impersonals in Italian. Italian Linguistics 1.11-31.
Contreras, Heles. 1976. A theory of word order with special reference to Spanish. Amsterdam: North-Holland Publishing Company.
Cooray, Mahinda. 1967. The English passive voice. English Language Teaching 21.203-210.
Cunha, Celso F. da. 1970. Gramática do português contemporâneo. Belo Horizonte: Editora Bernardo Álvares S.A.

Daneš, František. 1964. Sentence intonation from a functional point of view. Word 16.34-54.
Daneš, František. 1966. A three-level approach to syntax. Travaux Linguistiques de Prague 1.225-240.
Daneš, František. 1967. Order of elements and sentence intonation. In: To honor Roman Jakobson. Janua Linguarum (Series Maior) 31. The Hague: Mouton.
Daneš, František. 1968. Some thoughts on the semantic structure of the sentence. Lingua 21.55-69.
Daneš, František. 1970. One instance of Prague School methodology: Functional analysis of utterance and text. In: Method and theory in linguistics. Edited by Paul L. Garvin. The Hague: Mouton. 132-146.
Daneš, František, and Josef Vachek. 1966. Prague studies in structural grammar today. Travaux Linguistiques de Prague 1.21-31.
Dias, Augusto E. da Silva. 1959. Sintaxe histórica portuguêsa. 4th ed. Lisbon: Livraria Clássica Editora.
Di Pietro, Robert J. 1971. Language structures in contrast. Rowley, Mass.: Newbury House.
Ellison, Fred P., et al. 1971. Modern Portuguese. New York: Alfred A. Knopf.
Elson, Benjamin, and Velma Pickett. 1968. An introduction to morphology and syntax. Santa Ana, Calif.: Summer Institute of Linguistics.
Erades, P. A. 1950. His books don't sell. English Studies 31.155-157.
Erades, P. A. 1958-1959. Points in modern English syntax. English Studies 39.286 and 40.63-64.
Fillmore, Charles J. 1965. Indirect object constructions in English and the ordering of transformations. The Hague: Mouton.
Fillmore, Charles J. 1968. The case for case. In: Universals in linguistic theory. Edited by Emmon Bach and Robert Harms. New York: Holt, Rinehart and Winston. 1-88.
Firbas, Jan. 1959. Thoughts on the communicative functions of the verb in English, German, and Czech. Brno Studies in English 1.39-63.
Firbas, Jan. 1961. On the communicative value of the modern English finite verb. Brno Studies in English 3.79-104.
Firbas, Jan. 1964. From comparative word order studies. Brno Studies in English 4.111-126.
Firbas, Jan. 1965. A note on transition proper in functional sentence analysis. Philologica Pragensia 8.170-176.
Firbas, Jan. 1966a. On defining the theme in functional sentence analysis. Travaux Linguistiques de Prague 1.267-280.
Firbas, Jan. 1966b. Non-thematic subjects in contemporary English. Travaux Linguistiques de Prague 2.239-256.
Fries, Charles C. 1945. Teaching and learning English as a foreign language. Ann Arbor: University of Michigan Press.

Gaaf, W. van der. 1930. The passive verb accompanied by a preposition. English Studies 12.1-24.

Garvin, Paul L. 1963. Czechoslovakia. In: Current trends in linguistics 1. Edited by T. Sebeok. The Hague: Mouton. 499-511.

Gleason, H. A. 1955 (1st ed.) and 1961 (rev. ed.). An introduction to descriptive linguistics. New York: Holt, Rinehart and Winston.

Goldin, Mark. 1968. Spanish case and function. Washington, D.C.: Georgetown University Press.

Gross, Maurice. 1968. L'emploi des modèles en linguistique. Langages 9.3-8.

Hadlich, Roger L. 1965. Lexical contrastive analysis. The Modern Language Journal 49.426-429.

Hall, Robert A., Jr. 1964. Introductory linguistics. Philadelphia: Chilton Books.

Hall, Robert A., Jr. 1972. Why a structural semantics is impossible. Language Sciences 21.1-6.

Halliday, M. A. K. 1967-1968. Notes on transitivity and theme in English. Journal of Linguistics 3.37-81, 199-244, and 4.179-216.

Halliday, M. A. K. 1970. Language structure and language function. In: New horizons in linguistics. Edited by John Lyons. Harmondsworth, England: Penguin Books.

Hamp, Eric P. 1968. What a contrastive grammar is not, if it is. In: Alatis (1968). 137-147.

Harris, Zellig. 1951. Structural linguistics. Chicago: The University of Chicago Press.

Harris, Zellig. 1955. From phoneme to morpheme. Lg. 31. 190-222.

Hasegawa, H. 1968. The passive construction in English. Lg. 44.220-243.

Hatcher, A. G. 1949. To get/be invited. Modern Language Notes 64.433-446.

Hatcher, A. G. 1956a. Syntax and the sentence. Word 12.234-250.

Hatcher, A. G. 1956b. Theme and underlying question. Two studies in Spanish word order. Word 12, Supplement No. 3.

Hill, L. A. 1963. The passive again. English Language Teaching 18.69-74.

Hockett, Charles F. 1958. A course in modern linguistics. New York: Macmillan.

Hutchins, John A. 1975. Use and frequency of occurrence of verb forms in spoken Brazilian Portuguese. Hispania 58.59-67.

Jacobs, Roderick A., and Peter S. Rosenbaum. 1968. English transformational grammar. Waltham, Mass.: Blaisdell Publishing Co.

James, Carl. 1971. The exculpation of contrastive linguistics. In: Papers in contrastive linguistics. Edited by Gerhard Nickel. Cambridge, Mass.: Cambridge University Press. 53-68.

Jespersen, Otto. 1948. Essentials of English grammar. London: Allen and Unwin.
Jespersen, Otto. 1909-1949. A modern English grammar on historical principles. Vol. 4. London: Allen and Unwin (1961 edition).
Joos, Martin. 1968. The English verb: Form and meaning. 2nd ed. Madison: The University of Wisconsin Press.
Kac, M. B. 1969. Should the passive transformation be obligatory? Journal of Linguistics 5.145-147.
Katz, J. J., and J. Fodor. 1963. The structure of a semantic theory. Lg. 39.170-210.
Katz, J. J., and Paul M. Postal. 1964. An integrated theory of linguistic description. Research Monograph No. 26. Cambridge, Mass.: The MIT Press.
Katz, J. J., and Edwin Martin, Jr. 1967. The synonymy of actives and passives. The Philosophical Review 76.476-491.
Kirkwood, H. J. 1969. Aspects of word order and its communicative function in English and German. Journal of Linguistics 5.85-107.
Kruisinga, E. 1927. Retained accusatives in passive sentences. English Studies 9.38-40.
Lacerda, Eulício F. de. 1966. Sintaxe do português contemporâneo. Rio de Janeiro: Editora Pongetti.
Lakoff, George. 1965. On the nature of syntactic irregularity. Report NSF-16, Mathematical Linguistics and Automatic Translation. Cambridge, Mass.: Computation Laboratory, Harvard University.
Lakoff, George. 1968. Instrumental adverbs and the concept of deep structure. Foundations of Language 4.4-29.
Lakoff, Robin. 1971. Passive resistance. In: Papers from the Seventh Regional Meeting of the Chicago Linguistic Society. Chicago: Chicago Linguistic Society. 149-161.
Langacker, Ronald W. 1970. Review of: Goldin (1968). Lg. 46.167-185.
Langacker, Ronald W., and Pamela Munro. 1975. Passives and their meaning. Lg. 51.789-830.
Lapa, M. Rodrigues. 1970. Estilística da língua portuguesa. 6th ed. Rio de Janeiro: Livraria Acadêmica.
Lee, W. R. 1968. Thoughts on contrastive linguistics in the context of language teaching. In: Alatis (1968). 185-194.
Lees, R. B. 1957. Review of: Chomsky (1957). Lg. 33.375-408.
Lees, R. B. 1960. The grammar of English nominalizations. Publications of the Research Center in Anthropology, Folklore, and Linguistics No. 12. Bloomington, Ind.: Indiana University.
Lees, R. B. 1964. On passives and imperatives in English. Gengo Kenkyu 46.28-41.
Lester, Mark. 1971. Introductory transformational grammar of English. New York: Holt, Rinehart and Winston.

Lo Cascio, Vincenzo. 1976. On 'linguistic variables' and primary object-topicalization in Italian. Italian Linguistics 1.33-75.

Longacre, Robert E. 1960. String constituent analysis. Lg. 36.63-88.

Lozano, Anthony G. 1970. Non-reflexivity of the indefinite 'se' in Spanish. Hispania 53.452-457.

Lozano, Anthony G. 1972. The indefinite 'se' revisited. Hispania 55.84-85.

Mathesius, Vilém. 1928. On linguistic characterology with illustrations from modern English. In: A Prague School reader in linguistics. Edited by Josef Vachek. Bloomington: Indiana University Press, 1964. 59-68.

Melo, J. Nelino. 1968. Estudos práticos de gramática normativa da língua portuguêsa. Rio de Janeiro: Bruno Buccini, editor.

Mihailović, Ljljana. 1963. Some observations on the use of the passive voice. English Language Teaching 17.77-81.

Mihailović, Ljljana. 1965. The agent in the passive construction. English Language Teaching 20.123-126.

McCawley, James. 1968a. Concerning the base component of a transformational grammar. Foundations of Language 4.243-269.

McCawley, James. 1968b. Review of: Current trends in linguistics, 3. Lg. 44.556-593.

McCawley, James. 1969. Meaning and the description of language. Kotoba no uchū 2.10-51.

McCawley, James. 1970. Where do noun phrases come from? In: Readings in English transformational grammar. Edited by Roderick A. Jacobs and Peter S. Rosenbaum. Waltham, Mass.: Ginn and Company.

McKerrow, R. B. 1922. English grammar and grammars. Essays and Studies 8.148-167.

Naro, Anthony J. 1976. The genesis of the reflexive impersonal in Portuguese. Lg. 52:4.779-810.

Newmark, L., and Reibel, D. 1968. Necessity and sufficiency in language learning. International Review of Applied Linguistics 6.145-161.

Nickel, Gerhard. 1971. Contrastive linguistics and foreign language teaching. In: Papers in contrastive linguistics. Edited by Gerhard Nickel. Cambridge, Mass.: Cambridge University Press. 1-16.

Palmer, Frank R. 1965. A linguistic study of the English verb. London: Longmans.

Pereira, Eduardo Carlos. Gramática expositiva. Curso superior. 19th ed., n.d.; 1st ed., 1907. Rio de Janeiro: Companhia Editora Nacional.

Perini, Mário A. 1976. A gramática gerativa. Introdução ao estudo da sintaxe portuguesa. Belo Horizonte: Editora Vigília Ltda.

Politzer, Robert L. 1972. Linguistics and applied linguistics: Aims and methods. Philadelphia: The Center for Curriculum Development.

Ribeiro, Ernesto Carneiro. 1955. Serões gramaticais ou nova gramática portuguesa. 6th ed. (1st ed. 1907) Bahia: Livraria Progresso Editora.

Sá Pereira, M. L. 1948. Brazilian Portuguese grammar. Lexington, Mass.: D. C. Heath.

Schmitz, John Robert. 1973. The linguistic flexibility of 'a gente' in Portuguese. Hispania 56.639-644.

Searle, John. 1972. Chomsky's revolution in linguistics. The New York Review of Books 18:12.16-24.

Seelye, H. N. 1966. The Spanish passive: A study in the relation between linguistic form and world view. Hispania 49.290-292.

Silveira, A. F. de Sousa da. 1940. Lições de português. 4th ed. Rio de Janeiro: Companhia Editora Nacional.

Stageberg, Norman C. 1971. An introductory English grammar. 2nd ed. New York: Holt, Rinehart and Winston.

Stanley, Julia P. 1975. Passive motivation. Foundations of Language 13:1.25-39.

Stockwell, Robert P., J. D. Bowen, and J. W. Martin. 1965. The grammatical structures of English and Spanish. Chicago: The University of Chicago Press.

Svartengren, H. 1948. 'Become' as an auxiliary for the passive voice. Moderna Sprak 42.272-281.

Svartvik, Jan. 1966. On voice in the English verb. The Hague: Mouton.

Sweet, Henry. 1898. A new English grammar. Vol. 1. Oxford: Clarendon Press.

Thomas, Earl. 1969. The syntax of spoken Brazilian Portuguese. Nashville: Vanderbilt University Press.

Vachek, Josef. 1966. The linguistic School of Prague: An introduction to its theory and practice. Bloomington: Indiana University Press.

Valesio, Paolo. 1971. The distinction of active and passive. Linguistic Inquiry 2.407-414.

Valesio, Paolo. 1976. Between Italian and French: The fine semantics of active versus passive. Italian Linguistics 1.107-144.

Vázquez Cuesta, Pilar, and M. A. Mendes da Luz. 1961. Gramática portuguesa. Madrid: Gredos.

Visão. São Paulo: Sociedade Editorial Visão Ltda.

Warburton, Irene. 1975. The passive in English and Greek. Foundations of Language 13.563-578.

Wardhaugh, R. 1970. The contrastive analysis hypothesis. TESOL Quarterly 4.123-130.

Weiner, E. Judith, and William Labov. 1978. Constraints on the agentless passive. Paper given at the Linguistic Society of America meeting.

Weinreich, Uriel. 1966. Explorations in semantic theory. In: Current trends in linguistics, 3. Edited by T. A. Sebeok. The Hague: Mouton. 395-477.
Wells, Rulon S. 1947. Immediate constituents. Lg. 23.81-117.
Whitehall, H. 1956. Structural essentials of English. New York: Harcourt Brace.
Zandvoort, R. W. 1960. A handbook of English grammar. London: Longmans, Green.
Ziff, Paul. 1966. The nonsynonymy of actives and passives. The Philosophical Review 75.226-232.

www.ingramcontent.com/pod-product-compliance
Lightning Source LLC
LaVergne TN
LVHW090809070826
844660LV00022B/1133

* 9 7 8 0 8 7 8 4 0 0 7 8 2 *